HOME SENSE

HOME SENSE

A Year-Round
Practical Guide
for the Homeowner

by the Washington Post
"Home Sense" columnist

MIKE McCLINTOCK

CHARLES SCRIBNER'S SONS   NEW YORK

Library of Congress Cataloging-in-Publication Data

McClintock, Michael, 1945–
  Home sense.

  1. Dwellings—Maintenance and repair—Amateurs' manuals.
I. Title.
TH4817.3.M34   1986   643'.7   86–15438
ISBN 0-684-18655-1
ISBN 0-684-18656-X (pbk.)

Published simultaneously in Canada by Collier Macmillan Canada, Inc.
Composition and manufacturing by The Haddon Craftsmen, Inc.,
Scranton, Pennsylvania
Designed by Helen Granger/Levavi & Levavi
First Edition

The essays in this book are adapted from articles that first appeared in
The Washington Post.

for Triny

CONTENTS

HOME SENSE

JANUARY

1 NEW IS NOT NECESSARILY BETTER ANYMORE:
Instead, Renovating an Older House May Prove the Best Bet

Compared to a new house with a high price tag and a high mortgage rate, many small, old, and slightly worn buildings with 7 percent

2 REMODELING THE BASEMENT:
It May Be the Cheapest Way to Add Living Space

One of the best bargains in living space is the basement. In many homes the space already has a foundation, a floor, walls and ceiling, even some heat, and, no doubt, a maze of pipes and wires to supply water and electricity. It may be slightly dark and damp and need

3 PUTTING THE PIECES TOGETHER:
The Shakers Were on to Something with Their Kit-Furniture Designs

Kit furniture was one of the Shakers' best ideas. Their most talented craftsmen designed and built prototypes. Then the furniture was taken apart, and exact replicas of every component were cut and shipped in neat bundles to settlements where a farmer or a teacher

4 WORKING WITH WALLBOARD:
The Material-of-Choice for New and Replacement Walls

Gypsum wallboard is used in over 90 percent of all new homes and apartment buildings. It's the standard wall and ceiling material in residential construction and serves as the surface for partition walls in most commercial buildings. Last year, wallboard sales in the United

Indoor Projects

mortgages can show unexpected potential. Renovation and improvement work has always taken a backseat to new construction. But there may be more value in an older home than meets the eye.

remodeling, but it may cost less to transform it into an attractive living space than it will to start from scratch with new construction.

without woodworking skills could put the pieces back together. The sensible system that made quality furniture widely available in Shaker settlements is still used today by several small firms making historically accurate reproductions of classic furniture pieces.

States and Canada for new construction and remodeling work totaled twenty billion square feet. That's over a million acres of wallboard, an area approximately the size of Delaware.

1

NEW IS NOT NECESSARILY BETTER ANYMORE

Instead, Renovating an Older House May Prove the Best Bet

When mortgage rates approached 20 percent a few years ago, renovation was a necessary alternative to new construction. Faced with a twofold, or even threefold, increase in rates, many small, old, and slightly worn buildings with 7 percent mortgages started to show unexpected potential. But in many ways renovation and improvement work has always taken a backseat to new construction. Almost by definition "improvement" implies some deficiency that needs correcting, while "new" promises a trouble-free home.

Splashy magazine stories covered trendy residential architecture, not inner-city rehabs. Home-improvement loans were often more expensive than loans for new construction. Even some union pay scales differentiated between what's called "new work" and "old work," for example, paying more for painting beams and bare plaster walls in buildings under construction than for repainting apartments in existing buildings.

But now renovation and improvement is the equal of new construction in every way. Ever-rising costs of materials, labor, land,

Applying cedar shakes is one recently rediscovered alternative to covering up chronic repaint problems with aluminum or vinyl siding.

and financing have forced home builders to cut back in all departments to keep new houses relatively affordable. And more buyers have become aware of these trends to "minimal" construction that often do not compare favorably with methods and materials used twenty-five years ago. New homes may be more energy efficient but over the years may be less durable than older homes that are often described as "overbuilt." New is not necessarily better.

Renovation work is also receiving the publicity it deserves, in special-interest publications such as *The Old House Journal,* covering only forty-five-year-old (or older) homes, and in the press generally. Manufacturers who have traditionally concentrated on the "new" markets (every new home needs a truckload of fixtures, furnishings, and appliances) are beginning to readjust their sights. A recent report titled, "Renovation's Rewards: A 'Hidden' Construction Market Pays Off," prepared by the Sweet's Division of McGraw-Hill Information Systems Co., indicates that 60 percent of the nation's residential and commercial buildings are over twenty-two years old. They need regular repair and improvement work.

The Sweet's report also confirms a suggestion made by several industry analysts in the last two years—that total expenditures for renovation work now surpass total expenditures for new construction. Sweet's used many sources to prepare a statistical profile of the renovation industry, including federal agencies and several trade periodicals and trade associations. Here are a few of the highlights.

- From the Department of the Interior. From 1983 to 1984 there was a 19 percent increase in rehabilitation projects approved for special tax incentives, an all-time high since the incentive program started in 1977.
- From *Commercial Renovation.* The magazine projects final figures for 1984 will show a commercial improvement market of almost $70 billion.
- From *Qualified Remodeler.* Magazine surveys estimate residential remodeling expenditures are close to $50 billion a year.
- From the Department of Housing and Urban Development. Long-term records show remodeling and renovation expenditures as only 20 percent of total construction costs in 1960, as 33 percent by 1970, and as 42 percent by 1980.
- From *Interiors.* A survey of interior designers in 1984 found more than half of all design work concentrated in office remodeling, as 60 percent of corporate clients decided to work on their existing headquarters rather than move and build from scratch.

Renovation has overtaken new construction in residential and commercial markets. It's not surprising that when the employee stays in the same house instead of moving, the employer stays in the same office building or factory. Sociologists may argue about which group didn't move first. But the point is that mortgage rates, neighborhood stability, and other factors are common interests of both groups.

Designing and building your own house may always have a special allure, like being fitted for a custom-tailored suit instead of buying off the rack. But the Sweet's report marks a turning point away from the standard American dream of owning your own new home to the more realistic, although certainly difficult, task of buying, improving, and maintaining an existing building. This alternative is financially more realistic but also a response to changing life-styles and demographics. The report includes three key reasons for the fundamental shift away from new construction to renovation.

1. Homeowners who traditionally "traded up" (cashed in their appreciated value in home equity to buy a bigger house) are not willing to trade in 6, 7, and 8 percent conventional mortgages for 11 or 12 percent loans, much less 15–20 percent rates. Instead, they add on to the existing low-rate house.
2. An increased emphasis on stability makes homeowners less likely to change school districts or extend commuting time by moving.
3. As rising costs of new construction are partially counteracted with shrinking floor plans, older but larger homes become very appealing by comparison. This appeal is heightened by a growing appreciation of handcrafted construction details, soundproof plaster walls, features such as thick, high-quality hardwood floors too expensive to duplicate in typical new homes, and established landscaping.

But perhaps the most interesting finding in the report is not about buildings or projects but about the people who are making the improvements—the owners. David M. Sauer, publisher of *Qualified Remodeler*, puts it this way: "You're not going to see cheap doors and windows and lock sets in a renovation project." As opposed to the routine, hold-the-line repair and maintenance work usually associated with home ownership, the report found a special emphasis on "doing it right," using first-quality, energy-efficient, and durable methods and materials.

JUST ASK

Q How can I keep crayon marks and dirty handprints on the wall of my child's room from showing through when I repaint?

A When children's "artwork" (or grease stains around a kitchen stove or stains with a brown asphalt trace from a roof leak, for instance) reappear through a fresh coat of paint, it's called bleeding. And even high-quality paints, latex or oil, can't completely bury discolorations in one coat. Professional painters use a pigmented white shellac, nicknamed "stain killer"; it's quick drying, with tremendous hiding power. But make sure you ask for pigmented white shellac, which is a white color; plain old white shellac (the one you don't want but might get by mistake) is actually clear.

I would sand down the crayon marks and wash the handprints with warm water and a detergent. Then brush on a coat of the stain killer, repaint, and think about investing in an easel and watercolors for the budding artist.

2

REMODELING THE BASEMENT

It May Be the Cheapest Way to Add Living Space

One of the best bargains in living space is the basement. In many homes the space already has a foundation, a floor, walls and ceiling, even some heat, and, no doubt, a maze of pipes and wires to supply water and electricity.

Your basement may be slightly dark and damp and need remodeling, but it will cost a lot less to transform it into an attractive living space than it will to contract new construction. (According to the National Association of Home Builders, the average cost per square foot of new single-family construction, not counting improvements to the lot, was $44.15 in 1985.)

In many cases, complete remodeling includes scaled-down versions of almost every step in new construction. Two areas are particularly critical in remodeling a basement: the concrete floor and the masonry walls (poured concrete but more often concrete block).

The easiest way to treat concrete floors is with masonry paint. Two coats over a clean, dry floor (in some color other than battleship gray) can make the room much more inviting, although even painted concrete is a heavy-duty, workroom-type floor.

If the floor stays dry year round, a more expensive but more comfortable solution is carpeting. Even thin, commercial-type grades over a foam backing will make the floor softer, warmer, and more suitable as a playroom or bedroom; it will also absorb sound that would reverberate off hard masonry surfaces.

On problem floors that collect condensation or are uneven, heavily cracked, or covered with peeling layers of old paint or tile, a sleeper system is often the best solution. Sleepers are 2-by-4s laid with the wide side down on the concrete, usually 16 inches center to center. Rigid insulating panels may be added between boards, and a vapor barrier laid across them, before a new plywood subfloor is nailed down.

This elaborate system is expensive and time-consuming but produces a warm, dry, resilient, and level floor. (The 2-by-4 sleepers can be adjusted, a process called "shimming," to make up for

A dry basement floor is the key to a variety of remodeling options, from tile to carpeting, that can be applied directly over the concrete.

discrepancies in the concrete.) You must plan ahead to determine how the raised floor level (1½ inches of 2-by-4 and at least ½ inch of plywood) will alter details around doors. Also, to prevent deterioration of the sleepers, which may be in contact with at least some moisture, builders often set them in a thin bed of tar or use specially treated timbers that resist rot.

Masonry paint is also an expedient solution for walls, although even a bright color may not disguise the distinctively basement-looking style of concrete blocks. If the wall was carefully built, truly in line and with mortar joints practically flush with surrounding blocks, a thick coat of masonry paint may just hide the joints, producing a stucco effect.

It is more likely that the basement walls were not neatly finished and were meant simply to serve as rough structural supports. That's one reason the most common remodeling treatment is nailing 1-by-2-inch furring strips on the wall, covered by a layer of wallboard or paneling. The furring strips bridge the little bumps and jags in the wall and the depressions at mortar joints.

This system is serviceable except that masonry nails used to hold the strips to the wall create a lot of holes. Above ground level this may not pose a problem. But if you are fortunate enough to have basement walls that do not leak, it doesn't make sense to puncture them. Granted, the nails don't protrude through the walls. But a lot of them, all in a row, can create a kind of fault line that attracts structural stress. It's like a tiny snag in a stocking that can turn into a full-length run.

For not too much more money (compensated by reduced labor time), 1-by-2-inch furring can be replaced by 2-by-2-inch studding consisting of a 2-by-2-inch stud along the floor, another along the ceiling, joined by 2-by-2s set 16 inches from center to center. Two-by-two's are used in place of conventional 2-by-4s because the wall does not support anything; it only holds the wallboard or panel surface. The main benefit is that the complete 2-by-2 frame can be attached to the concrete floor with only a few nails (or none at all if the frame is set in a bed of construction adhesive) and nailed to the wooden floor joints of the house (the ceiling of the remodeled basement). Individual studs need not be nailed into the wall.

Using 2-by-2s also provides a bit more room for insulation than thin fiberglass batts or rigid styrene panels. Cover that assembly with a vapor barrier of plastic sheeting before applying the new surfacing material. This will keep interior moisture from working through the new wall and condensing on the masonry where it would be in contact with the frame and the insulation and cause deterioration.

JUST ASK

Q I need to refinish the wood paneling that lines our family room, but I'm worried about potentially harmful fumes from synthetic sealers and finishes. Aren't there alternatives?

A Available information shows that only a few building materials have been proved hazardous to health, namely asbestos, some ureaformaldehyde foam insulation, various pesticides, and some wood preservatives. Very little is known about the cumulative effects of glues, plastics, synthetic fibers, and other materials, particularly when even marginal effects are magnified inside tightly constructed, energy-efficient homes. Until this issue receives more attention, there will be little incentive for manufacturers to offer completely nontoxic products.

One West German firm, LIVOS Development and Research Co., offers a complete line of nontoxic wood finishes, including oils, waxes, shellacs, polishes, stains, lacquers, and even wood preservatives and wall paints. None of the products generates toxic fumes. All are made of natural materials such as plant oils and tree resins and are safe for people, animals, and even plants.

These products are distributed by Woodpecker's Tools Inc., 614 Aqua Fria St., Santa Fe, NM 87501. The company sends a complete catalog for $1 (free with any order) and provides a toll-free phone number for inquiries and orders (800-621-2591). It's an interesting alternative and worth investigating.

3

PUTTING THE PIECES TOGETHER

The Shakers Were on to Something with Their Kit-Furniture Designs

Kit furniture was one of the Shakers' best ideas. The most talented craftsmen designed and built prototypes. Then the furniture was taken apart, and exact replicas of every component were cut and shipped in neat bundles to settlements where a farmer or teacher without woodworking skills could put the pieces back together.

The sensible system that made quality furniture widely available in Shaker settlements is still used today by several small firms making historically accurate reproductions of classic Shaker Colonial furniture.

Major furniture pieces in kit form generally cost 50–60 percent of their store-bought counterparts. Materials are clear pine, solid maple, oak, cherry, and mahogany, not skimpy veneers glued over flake-board panels. Joints are traditional mortise and tenon instead of nuts and bolts. And kit buyers have the enjoyment and satisfaction of assembling and finishing quality furniture without struggling over complex carpentry.

Typical reproduction kits require some woodworking skills—

The rocker from Cohasset Colonials and the Shaker table from Shaker Workshops are reproductions of museum pieces produced in kit form.

not complex measuring and cutting but an understanding of furniture assembly, a restrained and tidy use of glue, and the patience to sand imperfections before finishing. For example, rungs on a chair kit may not fit smoothly into the leg-piece holes; even minor changes in humidity can make wood swell enough to disrupt a perfect match. Light sanding generally corrects the problem. Care with glue is needed to prevent excess from clogging the raw grain of exposed surfaces, preventing equal penetration of stain and creating a blotchy finish.

Most kit-furniture companies offer a wide selection of pieces, from large cabinets with over a hundred components to simple candle holders with only four or five parts. It's wise to start small. Call the kit company for details about the item you select from their catalog. Make sure no special tools or skills are required for assembly. Generally, no more than a hammer and screwdriver is required; on some larger pieces, clamps not ordinarily found in household toolboxes may be needed.

On both simple and complex kits these basic guidelines will help.

• Check all parts for cracks and warping and be sure every part is in the package.

- Read the instructions several times, matching kit pieces with the terminology used in the text.
- Dry fit (assemble without glue) all parts, sanding where necessary to make them fit smoothly.
- Leave plenty of time for assembly and finishing; don't hurry.

Few assembly instructions are as helpful as they could be—maybe because they are prepared by people too familiar with the kits. Illustrations may show front and side views, like an architect's blueprint, instead of three-dimensional pictorial views found in how-to magazines. The texts often move quickly from one step to the next, failing to anticipate obvious questions—confusion between two similar parts, which end is up, and such. That's why several readings and complete dry assembly is crucial. If you get stuck, call the manufacturer. As a rule, they are accessible, ready to help, and quite friendly.

Here are case-history reports on three representative pieces of kit furniture.

- Shaker Dining Chair. Assembled and finished, it costs approximately $250; in kit form, $125. The back of the chair is roughly 40 inches high; the seat is 21 inches wide by 17 inches deep. The Shaker Workshops No. 5 rock-maple armchair arrives in twelve pieces already sanded silky smooth. The back legs, slats, and rungs are shipped assembled. Dry fitting shows that several connecting rungs must be sanded to fit snugly into the leg-piece holes.

  Assembly is straightforward and takes less than an hour. Some finesse is needed to fit the assembled back because all the connecting rungs must drop into their corresponding holes at the same time. But the chair finds its own shape very well. There is no play in the joints, so it is clear what position to leave the back in as the glue sets.

  This kit comes with traditional Shaker chair tapes (1-inch-wide heavy fabric, available in several colors), woven to form a comfortable seat and back after the chair's frame is sealed. It's time-consuming to weave carefully, but the work isn't difficult. In fact, the repetition and slow but steady progress are very satisfying.

  Overall, this is an easy piece despite its scale. All details, including seat size, the unique splay of rear posts, and the curve of back rails, have been reproduced from originals built at the Shaker settlement in Mount Lebanon, N.Y.

- Eighteenth-Century Basin Stand. Assembled and finished, it costs approximately $425; in kit form, $139. The stand is 36 inches tall, with a 12-inch diameter top ring designed to hold a basin. The Bartley Collection basic stand, available in solid mahogany or cherry, reproduces a fashionable piece of bedroom furniture (circa 1760) designed to hold a washbowl and water pitcher, with a tiny triangular drawer for soap.

    Base legs are easily jointed with strong double dowels; some careful gluing and clamping is needed on the intricate upper section and drawer. Bartley includes a type of band clamp for the upper section, which didn't work too well for me. I substituted nylon cord with cardboard pieces to protect corners—tightened like a tourniquet—during gluing.

    The Bartley kit includes a color-matched paste filler for glue and wood that is easily sanded and accepts stain well. A paste stain and varnish can be combined to create various shades, and successive coats produce a deep and lustrous finish. Final sanding is a bit tedious, not because the pieces are rough but because vertical and horizontal grains are opposed on posts and connecting panels. Sanding with the grain requires controlled strokes and careful attention.

    Overall, this piece is more challenging than the Shaker chair simply because it is more ornate and has smaller pieces. A pewter bowl is available to fit the wooden ring.

- Seven-Drawer Chest. The chest is only available in kit form, for approximately $300. (For comparison, the firm's stunning rolltop desk is $669 in kit form; $1,389 assembled and finished.) The Craftsman's Corner oak chest is 20 inches wide, 20 inches deep, and 52 inches tall. The chest has about a hundred components, thankfully all coded, stamped, and keyed to the instructions.

    Assembly is accomplished in stages, as sections are built by gluing thin oak panels into grooves in solid connecting pieces. Joining completed side and back sections with four-draw dividers into a complete frame is an awkward business without large clamps. The large panels are a handful, and no matter how accurately they are assembled, final adjustments for a proper overall fit are inevitable. This is true on all large pieces where firm pressure is needed to overcome natural, if slight, irregularities in the wood.

    Oak-front drawers are assembled with lock joints, a modification of dovetail joinery that keeps the panel in place without clamps. Other helpful features include predrilled holes aligned for the drawer guides, eliminating minor measuring errors that can make drawers stick in their tracks.

Overall, this major piece requires some familiarity with woodwork assembly, and four or more 2-foot bar clamps make assembly easier and more accurate. All hardware, including drawer pulls and sandpaper, is included. Glue and stain are not provided. This is a heavy-duty, durable, solid oak cabinet, fully precut but best suited for real woodwork enthusiasts, at a very reasonable price.

Most kit manufacturers send catalogs on request. You can find their ads in how-to magazines. For catalogs from the three representative kit makers illustrated here, write: Shaker Workshops, P.O. Box 1028, Concord, MA 01742 (taped-back arm chair); The Bartley Collection Ltd., 121 Schelter Rd., Prairie View, IL 60069 (basin stand); and Craftsman's Corner, P.O. Box AP, Dept. 1PS, Des Moines, IA 50302 (seven-drawer chest).

JUST ASK

Q All the houses in my development have aluminum wiring. Some of my neighbors have called in electricians because they are worried about a fire hazard. Others tell me not to worry. Who's right?

A You should be worried enough to have the wiring checked by an electrician. When aluminum wiring is connected to light switches and outlets intended for more conventional copper wire systems, there is a fire hazard. Like oil and water, exposed aluminum wire leads and copper terminals don't mix. First, the different metals expand and contract at different rates when heated. Second, as exposed aluminum oxidizes, it resists current flowing through the connection and produces heat. (If your switch or outlet cover plate feels warm to the touch you should call an electrician immediately.) Between the heat and the unequal expansion and contraction, one of the wires may work loose. And that's dangerous.

Ask your electrician about "pigtailing," a process of heat shrinking short lengths of copper wire between the aluminum (which will be completely insulated) and the connection terminals at switches and outlets.

4

WORKING WITH WALLBOARD

The Material-of-Choice for New and Replacement Walls

Gypsum wallboard, also known as drywall, plasterboard, and Sheetrock (a U.S. Gypsum Co. trade name), is used in over 90 percent of all new houses and apartment buildings. It's the standard wall and ceiling material in residential construction and serves as the surface for partition walls in most commercial buildings.

Last year, sales in the United States and Canada for the three basic wallboard applications—new residential, new commercial, plus repair and remodeling work—totaled 20 billion square feet. That's over a million acres of wallboard, an area approximately the size of Delaware.

Years ago, when labor costs were not the overwhelming factor in the price of housing, plaster was the standard interior surfacing material. Now it's relegated to being one of the pleasant bonuses of living in an older home or in an apartment building where lofty ceilings are outlined with intricate plaster cornices. Plastering is a disappearing trade but not because of problems with the material.

*The basic ingredients
of a drywall job
include ½-inch thick
4×8-foot sheets, nails,
knife, hammer,
spackle knife, and
joint compound.*

Plaster is hard, strong, easily repaired, readily painted or papered, fire resistant, and effective at reducing sound transmission. It's almost the ideal building material. Its only shortcoming is that it must be applied over a rigid structural frame to avoid surface cracking. Minimal, modern framing, designed to get the most use from the least amount of lumber, is often not rigid enough. Also, plaster is time-consuming to install and takes a long time to dry.

In a way, wallboard is like portable, predried plaster. It can be installed quickly, and after a three-coat taping job to fill and smooth seams between boards and cover nail heads, looks just as good as a plaster wall. Wallboard is manufactured in many different sizes, thicknesses, and joint configurations, with special chemical treatments and additives to fit a variety of architectural, structural, and practical demands. Finally, while plaster work is becoming a highly specialized restoration handcraft, installing wallboard is a reasonable do-it-yourself job.

Standard wallboard panels are 4 feet wide, ½ inch thick, and 8 feet long; 9-, 10-, 12-, and 14-foot lengths can be ordered to fit wall to wall and minimize the number of seams. Other thicknesses include ¼ inch for resurfacing work, ⅜ inch for resurfacing and double-layer construction, and ⅝ inch for new, heavy-duty walls.

Tapered edges are built into the long sides of the panels so that the seams are slightly recessed. This allows layers of tape and joint compound covering the seams to connect the panels into a uniformly flat wall.

Although standard panels work well in all rooms, two special types are worth considering for particular areas. Water-resistant panels (often shortened to W/R on blueprints) include an asphalt mix in the gypsum core and a chemical additive in the surface paper. These green-tinted panels should be used as a base for adhesive-applied tile and generally to reduce deterioration from moisture in kitchens, baths, and utility rooms.

Fire-retardant panels (generally referred to as FC panels) also have a specially formulated core that increases the amount of time wallboard stays intact when exposed to fire. These panels are a worthwhile alternative in furnace rooms and in kitchens (two likely sources of fire).

There are several crucial elements in wallboard installation, starting with the condition of the frame on which the panels are applied. Obviously, individual wall studs or ceiling joists should be solid and aligned so that the panels lie flat. What's not at all obvious is the amount of moisture in those timbers; the timbers may shrink and twist as they dry and damage taped seams and nails. Nail popping is probably the most common problem with wallboard.

Construction frames should be rated at 19 percent moisture content (or less). If you or your contractor come across an inordinantly heavy stud or joist, chances are it's loaded with excess moisture. Don't use it. Also, try to minimize the amount of time raw framing is exposed to the weather during construction or remodeling. But even well-built and relatively dry frames shrink a bit after a few heating seasons, often just enough to break the friction-holding power of nails.

Extensive testing by gypsum suppliers shows that long nails driven deeply into the wood frame protrude more than shorter nails when the wood dries. Since shorter nails have less holding power, special resin-coated nails with wide heads and a series of rings on the shank were developed. A 1¼-inch, ringed drywall nail is recommended for standard ½-inch panels.

Professionals go one step better by using drive screws, sharply pointed, Phillips-head fasteners that lock into wood framing with wide threads. Because of their tapered heads, they produce a neat dimple in the wallboard surface that is easily

filled with joint compound. The pros use special drills to set
these fasteners. But a do-it-yourselfer can take advantage of
this durable fastening system by using a Phillips-head bit in a
standard ¼-inch drill. It's worth a try, particularly if you don't
have the greatest track record with hitting nails on the head.

Planning the installation is also important. Generally, the rigid-
ness of panels can improve overall building strength most effectively when applied with the panels' longest side perpendicular to
the framing, that is, parallel to the floor. This way, each panel ties
many pieces of the frame together. But the most sensible plan is
to install the panels in a way that minimizes the number of taped
seams. If, for example, 4-by-12-foot panels can be maneuvered
into a 12-by-12-foot room with 8-foot ceilings, the walls can be
covered with only eight sheets. After ceiling and floor seams are
covered by molding, only four corners and one horizontal seam
around the room need taping. Big panels are unwieldy. But the
extra effort up front saves taping and spackling work later on.

The finishing process is actually three steps, called a three-coat
taping job. First, a narrow base coat of joint compound is spread
with a trowel over the seam, and a layer of paper joint tape is
embedded gently in the base coat and smoothed. Then, after drying and light sanding (if required), a wider, second coat of compound is applied to cover the tape and fill the depression at the
seam. After sanding again, apply a thin, wider finishing coat of
compound; and finally, sand lightly.

With practice, compound can be applied smoothly, without most
of the little cuts and ridges that require sanding. It helps to mix
the compound to an almost soupy consistency and to keep trowel
blades very clean. Inevitably, the last seam you tape will be the
fastest and probably the neatest.

Because gypsum wallboard is so widely used, product brochures are available at many lumberyards and home centers. For
a free illustrated brochure called "How to Apply Sheetrock Brand
Gypsum Panels to Existing Walls and Ceilings," send your request to U.S. Gypsum Co., Dept. 122-ZZ, 101 S. Wacker Dr., Chicago, IL 60606. The brochure covers fifteen basic installation
steps, forming and finishing inside and outside corners, planning,
measuring, estimating materials, and more, all in no-nonsense
how-to language.

JUST ASK

Q I'm using what the paint dealer calls a "masonry surfacer" over the concrete block walls of the cellar and a flat latex paint on the wallboard ceilings. Can I use the same roller for both jobs, or do I need a brush for the masonry?

A Look closely at the rollers in the paint store and you'll see that they are sold in different lengths and naps. That refers to the thickness of the roller mat—the surface that holds the paint. Fine-nap mohair rollers create a smooth surface. They would be a good selection for applying high-gloss oil paint to kitchen cabinets, for example.

For the rough-surfaced concrete block, you should use a similarly rough-surfaced roller. In the trade these wooly rollers are called "bulldozers," because they hold so much paint (even thick material like a masonry surfacer) and push it ahead of the roller like a bulldozer. The thick nap is needed to thoroughly coat all the little crevices in the block surface. On smooth walls fine-nap rollers leave a flat finish, and heavy-nap rollers leave a textured finish.

FEBRUARY

1 BUILT-IN APPLIANCES:
Today's Space-Saving Appliances Stand Out in a Crowd

You can't have too much closet or counter space. It's difficult to add closets without giving up expensive living space. But there is a relatively easy way to recapture counter space and increase efficiency in

2 TOLL-FREE TELEPHONE NUMBERS:
Help for Consumers Is Often Only a Phone Call Away

Toll-free numbers are being used increasingly as a tool to generate sales. They work for businesses and for consumers by providing access to accurate, up-to-date information in many areas, including appliance repair, real estate investment, product safety, insurance

3 ENERGY SAVERS:
Putting Your House on an Energy Diet

There are three basic approaches to saving energy: Use less fuel, retain more heat, and produce heat more efficiently. The most basic plan—one that works as well for dieters as for energy savers—is simply to consume less fuel. It's easy advice to offer. But several

4 APPLIANCE TROUBLESHOOTING:
Investigating and Solving Common Problems

Old refrigerators kept food cold. New refrigerators keep different types of food at different temperatures, make ice, supply ice water through the door, and more. Some new models even display temperatures in the various compartments on a door-mounted panel. But

Appliances

the kitchen and elsewhere: by using double-duty, space-saving appliances.

rates, and more. In 1978, 1.3 billion toll-free calls were made in the United States. Now, the rate is approaching 4 billion calls a year on close to 400,000 toll-free lines.

devices make cutting back and doing without relatively painless, and they save energy dollars.

while convenience features have proliferated on many types of appliances and energy efficiency has increased, many of the most common problems with appliances have not changed.

1

BUILT-IN APPLIANCES

Today's Space-Saving Appliances
Stand Out in a Crowd

Generally, you can't have too much closet or counter space. It's difficult to add closets because you have to give up living space to do it—a tough decision at today's high per-square-foot prices. But there is a relatively easy way to recapture counter space and increase efficiency in the kitchen and elsewhere: by using double-duty appliances.

In the broadest sense, double-duty means that the appliances accomplish more than you'd expect. And there are several kitchen appliances, big and small, that do the job.

The NuTone Food Center may be the ultimate double-duty appliance. It has been a staple since it was introduced in 1956 and seems somehow symbolic of the incredible, clean-countered spaciousness of "space-age" kitchens from the late 1950s and early 1960s—those "quaint" 20-by-30-foot center-island layouts seen weekly in the television homes of people like Ozzie and Harriet.

The Food Center motor is mounted out of sight, under the counter. Only a sleek, flush-mounted control panel shows on the counter surface. A food processor and mixer—fourteen different machines in all—can be plugged into the drive mechanism on the countertop panel. The idea is sensible: Buy a whole group of appliances, but only one set of controls and one motor to run them.

The drawbacks? You can use only one machine at a time, which is not much of a problem unless you're trying to run a restaurant. And you must use the appliances at the fixed spot on the counter where the Food Center is installed.

One of the most fully developed product lines of space-efficient appliances, Spacemakers, is made by General Electric. GE uses the space above counters the way real estate developers use the air rights above buildings: to create room for expansion.

GE recently introduced a line of slim-profile combinations of televisions, radios, clocks, and cassette recorders (incorporated into message centers). The Kitchen Companion Radio, for example, uses less than 3 inches of the space between counter and upper cabinet, presenting the radio dials, digital clock face, and controls, including a clock-timed outlet for other appliances and a few other nifty features, at a convenient height.

Running matching base trim across the kickspace of a dishwasher or other appliance provides a nice finishing touch on built-ins.

GE has also introduced a coffee maker and a microwave oven that mount just under upper cabinets. The first microwave units were monsters compared with the cabinet-depth models now available. But the most innovative product in this line is a specially shaped dishwasher designed to fit into the cabinet space directly under the sink.

Usually a wasteland of drainpipes, oversized baking pans, boxes of detergent, and all manner of oddball storage containers, the nearly dead space under the sink is cleverly used by this peculiar humpbacked dishwasher. A shallow sink and drain outlet (6 inches deep from counter to drain) must be used in a cabinet at least 24 inches deep.

Another great space saver, particularly useful in apartments, is the over-and-under washer-dryer combination now offered by many manufacturers. While most apartments don't have room for full-size, side-by-side laundry appliances, many have an available corner or small closet for these two-in-one, 24-inch-wide units. And they may pay for themselves by saving trips to the Laundromat.

The self-venting electric range is another classic—popularized by the Jenn-Air Co. and now offered by several other manufacturers. These ranges come in many shapes and sizes, with all kinds of features, but are outstanding because of their integral venting system. Plug-in burner units, a griddle, even a grill, can be used without depositing grease and grime on every surface between the stove and a typical wall-mounted exhaust fan.

The drawbacks? These ranges are expensive, and the powerful fan removes warm air in winter along with the grime. But venting on the spot reduces many kinds of cleaning and maintenance—on paint, plastic laminates, tile, and grout. Being able to grill over charcoal-type elements indoors, during the winter, is another bonus.

For referrals to NuTone dealers carrying the Food Center, call toll-free, 800-543-8687. For information on General Electric Spacemaker appliances, call the GE Answer Center's toll-free number, 800-626-2000. For details on Jenn-Air appliances, write Jenn-Air Co., 3035 N. Shadeland Ave., Indianapolis, IN 46226 (317-545-2271).

JUST ASK

Q How can we keep some humidity in the air during the heating season? A forced hot-air furnace and a wood stove make the house and our throats dry as a bone.

A When it is 20°F outside with 60 percent relative humidity, heating inside air to 70° F reduces relative humidity below 10 percent. That's dry enough to shrink floorboards, open glued joints in furniture, and make your nose and throat feel like sandpaper. In order to feel comfortable (40 or 50 percent relative humidity will suit most people), you must add moisture continually. On a forced hot-air furnace, an automatic humidifier can be fitted to the plenum, the large sheet-metal chamber directly over the combustion chamber of the furnace. It's generally a one-day job for well-organized do-it-yourselfers.

Different manufacturers offer variations on this basic system: Water is fed to a reservoir in the humidifier where it is absorbed by sponge-like evaporator pads dipping in and out of the water while a small fan blows air over the moisture-laden pads and into the supply ducts. Leave a cast-iron kettle or heat-tempered crockery pot filled with water on top of a wood stove to add moisture in that particularly warm and dry area.

2

HELP IS ONLY A PHONE CALL AWAY

The Growing Popularity of Toll-Free Numbers

In 1981, the Quaker Oats Co. put treasure maps in boxes of Cap'N Crunch cereal and asked consumers to call a toll-free 800 number to see if the message on their maps matched a prerecorded message, making them instant winners. Twenty-four million people called. And as a result of the promotion, Quaker Oats dramatically increased the sales and market share of its cereal.

Toll-free numbers are being used increasingly as a tool to generate sales. They work for businesses, and for consumers by providing access to accurate, up-to-date information in many areas other than breakfast cereal, including appliance repair, real estate investment, product safety, insurance rates, and more.

In 1978, 1.3 billion toll-free calls were made in the United States. Now the rate is approaching 4 billion calls a year on close to 400,000 toll-free lines. (Many are used by businesses and are not available to consumers.) National hotel chains, airlines, and other large corporations have widely publicized toll-free numbers that make it easy for consumers to buy their products and services. But many large and small firms staff their toll-free phones with experts who can provide valuable information.

Could Alexander Graham Bell have envisioned this kind of long-distance, electronic troubleshooting? Imagine a flashlight in one hand and a phone in the other as you peer into the maze of wires between the timer and the motor on your washing machine. A repairman is at the other end of an 800 number halfway across the country, scanning a schematic plan of the machine's wiring on a computer terminal. The manufacturer's troubleshooter leads you through a checklist based on frequency of repair reports and on experience gleaned from problem-solving sessions with other consumers.

In most cases, problems are not unique to your machine (or whatever you're having trouble with), so that a solution may be found over the phone, eliminating an expensive, on-site service call. And since the service is free, it is a relief, not an expensive embarrassment, when the problem turns out to be something silly like a blown fuse or a loose plug.

From a consumer's point of view, it's convenient when companies advertise their toll-free numbers. But it's unlikely that you keep a record of them. AT&T has a toll-free information line for 800 numbers (800-555-1212), but it is useful only if you are searching for a particular manufacturer. The service is not set up to

There may not be a repairman on 800 lines such as GE's Answer Center, but computerized troubleshooting data can solve many problems.

provide general searches—for instance, if you have a question about the toxicity of a certain household chemical. But if you knew that the Environmental Protection Agency had a pesticide hotline, an information operator could provide the number.

Aside from starting a small file of toll-free numbers on subjects of particular interest, there are at least two other extensive sources of 800 listings. The *Money-Saving Toll-Free Phone Book* (Beekman House, $9.95) is a large-format, 352-page paperback with about sixteen hundred toll-free listings, including travel services, many government agencies, and firms dealing in everything from clothing and home furnishings to food and health services. It is a limited but broad selection that includes a synopsis of the service offered on each toll-free number.

AT&T publishes two toll-free directories: a consumer edition (78 pages, $6.75) and a business edition (202 pages, $8.75). Together, they include sixty-five thousand toll-free listings. The distinction between the two directories is difficult to pinpoint. Many sources are listed in both books, although the business edition includes some firms that supply products and services to other businesses, not to consumers. The toll-free directories can be ordered by calling 800-242-4634.

After the first printing a million free samples of the consumer edition were mailed to customers in an effort to publicize the directories. AT&T reports it is too soon to estimate the response, although overall toll-free number usage continues to increase. But it appears that many consumers are not aware of the directories or the fact that so many information sources are available over toll-free lines.

There should be an ever-increasing number of toll-free lines. Since the Federal Communications Commission ruled in favor of allowing single-line toll-free services, many small, specialized firms have discovered their merits. Previously, the two-line minimum (which cost around $37 per month) favored large companies that could afford the fees and deal with the increased volume of calls.

A few final tips on toll-free service may help you get the most out of this growing source of free information.

- It's often worth trying a toll-free number after normal business hours. Many national firms use an enhanced 800 service that automatically switches calls from offices in the East to offices in later time zones as the normal business day ends.

Increasing the workday from eight to eleven hours is good for business and makes it easier for consumers to call at their convenience.

- Home phone systems with an automatic redial feature can overcome the problem of reaching a busy toll-free number. These phones keep dialing until a connection is made. Using toll-free lines at off-peak hours also helps.
- Remember that waiting on hold, fuzzy connections, even abrupt disconnections, should be less troubling, because they are at the company's expense.

A special toll-free information number (800-855-1155) is available for hearing- or speech-impaired customers using teletype or other special communications systems.

JUST ASK

Q We have a vacation home about three hours north of the city but can't get there every weekend. I worry about break-ins, the sump pump, power failures, and who knows what else. Any suggestions?

A A small computerized box that ties into your phone may be the answer. It doesn't fry bacon and eggs, but it does handle just about everything else. The Sensaphone box monitors inside air temperature, upper and lower temperature limits that you program in, electrical power status, and interior noise level, from a burglar or fire alarm, for example. There are optional, remote sensors to monitor water level (at your sump pump), temperature-sensitive locations away from the box (at your furnace), and remote security devices.

But here's the good part. You can call your vacation-home telephone and listen to a computer-synthesized voice that provides a status report of every monitored condition. Better yet, you can program in four telephone numbers (your home in the city, your number at work, etc.) that the box will dial automatically and continuously until it gets an answer should any problems develop. So you can call the house, and the house (the Sensaphone) can call you.

Suggested retail is $250 (but shop around for a mail-order price closer to $200). For details, write Sensaphone, 101 Chester Rd., Swathmore, PA 19081; or you can sample the computer voice over the company's toll-free line, 800-228-8466.

3

ENERGY-SAVERS

Putting Your House on an Energy Diet

Saving energy is about as specific a process as dieting. In both cases there are hundreds of methods and philosophies. Some work well, while others are only harebrained schemes, even rip-offs. Consumers are faced with advice that ranges from restating the obvious advantages of insulating uninsulated walls to applying complicated scientific systems, formulas, R values, sun angles, and other technicalities.

There are three basic approaches to saving energy: use less fuel, retain more heat, and produce heat more efficiently. The most basic plan—one that works as well for dieters as for energy savers—is simply to consume less fuel. It's easy advice to offer. But cutting back and doing without often seems to be the least attractive option.

The second approach, retaining more heat in living spaces, consists of a battery of reasonably nontechnical and relatively low-cost home improvements. The jobs typically recommended in home-energy audits performed by utility companies include adding insulation to uninsulated areas, increasing ceiling insulation,

Setback thermostats save energy automatically (figure about 3 percent of heating costs for every degree of heat you do without).

installing vapor barriers (either foil-faced batts of insulation or plastic sheeting) to keep moisture out of wall cavities, adding air-infiltration barriers (a moisture-permeable, paperlike wrapping) under new siding, and a combination of caulking and weather-stripping to seal seams.

The seemingly endless list includes substantial tasks such as adding storm windows, two-panel replacement windows, or more temporary interior plastic for double glazing. Very small projects include fitting thin foam pads beneath switch and outlet cover plates to reduce drafts and heat loss.

Problems arise when consumers, attracted by the promise of a 3 percent fuel saving ("on average") for one improvement and a 5 percent saving for another, follow only two or three parts of a whole-house, energy-saving prescription. Caulking, weather-stripping, even adding insulation in only one part of the house, may produce marginal benefits unless a whole-house plan is followed.

Heat, like water, tends to flow along the path of least resistance. Expensive warm air does not oblige by resting against a recently insulated ceiling. Slowly but surely it will find its way through the remaining gaps in the weather-sealing system and out of the house.

Energy-saving percentage figures are guidelines. Don't take them literally. If the figures were completely accurate, it would be possible to implement enough projects to save more than 100 percent of your fuel costs—a neat trick.

The third approach to saving energy, producing heat more efficiently, is the riskiest. For some systems you have to spend quite a lot of money to save fuel costs. One of the most common questions (a question that first surfaced during the energy crisis of the mid-seventies) is whether to switch from oil to gas; people also ask when it makes sense to invest in a new heating system.

The deregulation of natural gas could make prices for that fuel as unpredictable as oil rates, although many industry analysts do not expect a dramatic and immediate price hike. Currently, oil prices are moderate, and supplies are relatively abundant; OPEC members continue to squabble, the U.S. Strategic Petroleum Reserve continues to grow, and U.S. consumers continue to use less fuel and use it more efficiently.

On a more practical level, gas combustion is cleaner than oil combustion and requires less furnace maintenance. Oil is delivered by truck, which is a problem for some homeowners with long driveways in snow country. Gas is fed through underground pipes. The cost of installing a gas line from the street main to the house can be a decisive factor in favor of oil.

Finally, the most efficient new furnaces are gas furnaces, pulse-combustion units that cost $3,500 and up for most homes but run at 90 to 95 percent efficiency. The only caveat concerns noise. Some people report that the pulse system sounds like a small airplane revving in the cellar.

Although there are many complicated methods, there's one practical way to judge the merits of fuel conversion and buying a new high-efficiency furnace. First, have the combustion efficiency of the existing system tested. Heating contractors can provide this service if your utility company cannot. If it is 75 percent or better (75 percent of the energy, and fuel cost, becomes usable heat; 25 percent becomes exhaust), and the furnace does not require regular and costly repairs, converting to a new system is not likely to be cost-effective.

Still, compare the existing efficiency (e.g., 75 percent) to the rating of a new system (which may be 90 percent). If you spend $1,000 per year on fuel and the new system is 15 percent more efficient, you should save approximately 15 percent on fuel costs, or $150 per year. If the new system costs $3,000, the savings will pay back the energy-saving investment in twenty years, at best, since the efficiency rating will deteriorate as the system ages. That's a rotten investment. But if you can upgrade from 60 to 90 percent efficiency for $3,000 and spend $2,000 a year on fuel, the roughly 30 percent saving (or $600) means a payback period of only five years. That's a great investment.

Thermostats that automatically set temperatures back are a much less expensive but potentially more productive investment. The units, which replace conventional thermostats, cost between $50 and $150, depending on complexity, and save fuel and money regardless of furnace efficiency. Most units in the $100 range automatically lower thermostat settings for at least two separate and adjustable blocks of time during a twenty-four-hour time period. The idea is to produce heat only when people are in the house, while saving roughly 3 percent of total heating costs per degree of setback on the thermostat.

Of course, the last person to bed can lower the setting manually. But then the first person up in the morning freezes until the house warms up again—not a nice way to start the day. Setback or clock thermostats can be programmed to reinstate the standard 68°F setting fifteen minutes or so before the first alarm clock rings.

These systems save the most money in households with regular schedules and in homes where everyone leaves for work or school during the day. In these cases it is possible to set the heat back from 68° F to 53° F (15 degrees) for eight hours during the day and eight hours overnight. A 15-degree setback for two-thirds of the day saves two-thirds of the 3 percent degree rule (in this case, 2 percent times 15 degrees, or 30 percent of heating costs). At that rate of saving, and with an annual fuel bill of $1,000, even an elaborate, digital-clock thermostat for $150 would pay for itself in six months.

JUST ASK

Q Our refrigerator is making ice on the bottom of the freezer compartment. We defrosted manually once, but the ice is back again. Does this kind of problem require a service call, or is there a less expensive solution?

A This could be caused by a broken freezer fan or a problem with the switch that operates it. As the freezer door opens and closes, the switch often becomes water damaged or simply wears out. Open the door and depress the switch to see if the fan runs. If it doesn't, you'll need a service call to replace the fan or switch. Ask the service representative to check the switch first. It's the likely culprit and less expensive to replace than the fan.

Your problem could also be a clogged drain line, and you can fix that. On most models, water produced by automatic defrosting runs through a hose or metal tube starting from a drain in the freezer-compartment floor and ending in a drain pan beneath the refrigerator where it should evaporate. Defrost manually once more to get at the drain hole in the freezer floor (after unplugging the refrigerator, of course), then flush the line with hot water. A squeeze-top baster works well for flushing the line and can provide enough pressure to dislodge bits of food or paper causing the clog. Also, make sure the door gaskets are clean and tight to keep warm room air (which can produce frost) out of the compartment.

4

APPLIANCE
TROUBLESHOOTING

Investigating and Solving
Common Problems

Old refrigerators kept food cold. New refrigerators keep different types of food at different temperatures, make ice, supply ice water through the door, and more. One 1985 model even displays temperatures in the various compartments on a door-mounted panel. But while convenience features have proliferated on many types of appliances and energy efficiency has increased, many of the most common problems with appliances have not changed.

"Frost-Free" Refrigerator Frost

Every time you open the refrigerator or freezer door, some of the warm air in the house will mix with some of the cold air in the refrigerator. And when a warm front meets a cold front, it rains. In a refrigerator the result is frost, which can build and build until the doors must be left open long enough to melt the giant snow cones stuck to the walls (and to all the frozen food, too).

To eliminate this chore, almost all refrigerators use a heater;

that's right, a heater. In a typical frost-free unit a set of evaporator coils and a defrost heater are built into the partition between
refrigerator and freezer sections. A fan circulates air from the
compartments through the coils.

Although the defrosting is supposed to be automatic, it is not
uncommon for these refrigerators to accumulate frost, particularly after a few years of service. If large amounts of frost appear
in only a few days, the problem is likely to be an inoperative
evaporator fan (usually located on the back wall of the freezer
compartment). The fan motor may need to be replaced. This is
likely to be the first diagnosis offered by the appliance repairman.

But the problem may be caused by the fan switch, a small, much
less expensive component. It is activated as the freezer door opens
and closes. (You have to open the door and depress the switch by
hand to check if the fan is running.) On many side-by-side refriger-
ator-freezers this switch is near the floor, so that any excess
moisture, spills from refilled ice trays, or melting ice cream can
easily foul the switch. The unit can be replaced by prying out the
switch and attaching the wire leads (after unplugging the refrigerator) to a replacement.

*New appliances such
as this Sears
refrigerator display
current operating
and temperature data
on a monitor built
into the door.*

On machines several years old, more gradual accumulations of frost are likely to be caused by worn door gaskets. Magnets inside the pliable rubber gaskets force the door-mounted seals against the refrigerator. But when the gaskets are dirty, the magnets lose effectiveness. And in time the gaskets lose their elasticity and simply wear out.

Test the seal by closing strips of newspaper in the door. If they tear when you try to pull them out, the seal is tight enough. But if they pull out easily without tearing, a set of replacement gaskets will save energy and prevent frost buildup.

Clogged Waste Disposers

Advertisements for waste disposers (the cleaned-up name for a kitchen garbage grinder) may suggest that the machines will "eat" just about anything. Chances are if it's edible to you the machine will oblige. It may not do as well on the implements you eat with. A fork, a particularly tough chicken bone, and other stray objects can jam the flywheel, bringing the disposer to a grinding (sorry) halt.

Before the motor can burn itself out struggling against the immovable object, an overload switch will turn it off. Some manufacturers have anticipated this problem and provide a switch to reverse the flywheel rotation. It can be activated after the motor cools and the overload button is reset. On other models you must unplug the appliance, then attack the problem with a high-tech, troubleshooting tool—a broomstick handle. (Never reach down into the machine, even when the power is disconnected.)

Obviously you shouldn't try to beat the machine to death with this stick. Simply apply pressure to free the flywheel. If that doesn't work, try using a long-handled pliers to pull directly on the object causing the blockage.

Jamming from all but the largest and strongest objects can be minimized by letting the unit self-feed. Don't cram material into the drain or pack in waste before starting the machine. Just before, during, and for fifteen or twenty seconds after operating the disposer, supply a full-strength jet of cold water. This lubricates the operation, congeals grease so that it does not stick and accumulate in the mechanism, and flushes the pipes clean after grinding is complete.

Boosting Water-Heater Efficiency

During the winter, heat escaping from a hot-water tank is not exactly wasted. Granted, if it is not keeping the water warm, it may not be doing its job. But if it helps to warm the furnace room, it's not lost the way it would be out an open window. In the summer, all this changes.

Heat escaping from the tank causes inefficient water heating and adds to the cooling and ventilation load. This can be costly, considering that water heating accounts for 15 percent of residential energy consumption. (An average family uses about 100 gallons of hot water a day.) There are several steps that can make the water hotter without turning up the thermostat.

Adding a blanket of insulation to the heater is an easy do-it-yourself project. Insulation kits generally costing $20 or less are precut to fit snugly around the tank (not over the thermostat or pilot-light access door). They improve on the built-in tank insulation, which may be minimal on pre-energy-crisis heaters and reduce the amount of heat lost through the tank walls.

After several years of operation (or every year for homes using private well water that may have a high mineral content), flush out the tank. All water heaters have a drain cock near the base for this purpose. Attach a garden hose to the threaded fitting, open the valve, and empty the tank outside or down a house drain. This helps to clear sediment and other deposits that are carried in with the fresh water supply and settle at the bottom of the tank.

A bad case of sediment buildup will produce a percolating sound when the heater fires up. Since the sediment settles between the heat source and most of the water, it makes strange noises and wastes energy as superheated water bursts through the sediment into cooler water above. It's one thing to pay for hot water; another to continually reheat a pile of sediment.

Water-heater efficiency can be dramatically improved by adding an automatic setback timer. Until recently, these devices were available only for conventional wall thermostats controlling a furnace. Now the same principle of automatically reducing demand according to individual needs has been applied to both gas and electric water heaters.

One of the first such units, called Qwaterback (made by the Paragon division of AMF), is installed directly over existing water-heater thermostats. It can be programmed to turn down the water temperature at midnight, for example, then turn it back up a half hour before anyone gets out of bed. The company promises savings of up to $50 a year.

Sluggish Washing Machines

No one calls a clothes washer an automatic washing machine anymore. The novelty of tossing in the clothes and detergent and walking away while the machine churns through its many cycles wore off decades ago.

The automation is very convenient but often very fragile. Even a few minute pieces of grit can rearrange the programmed sequence of events. For instance, when grit clogs the filtering screens set into the water-supply hoses, the rate of flow is reduced. That means machines with a water-level switch may take forever to fill, and machines controlling water fill by cycling a timer will start washing before enough water has entered.

To follow a basic principle of making repairs (to try the most simple, least expensive solution first), turn off the water-inlet valves where your plumbing pipes end and the flexible hoses supplying water to the machine begin. Then unscrew the water-inlet hoses where they connect to the machine. Just inside the hot and cold fittings on the machine are two thin filter screens. Pry them out carefully. Tiny pieces of grit can be washed off under a tap. Use a soft toothpick to dislodge stubborn pieces.

If changing the water-temperature controls does not have any effect on the water entering the machine or if water continues to fill after the machine is full, the problem is likely in the solenoid valve. Although a service call may be required to fully test a solenoid valve, overfilling can be caused by a stuck valve plunger.

The solenoid is like an electrically triggered faucet. It operates a spring-loaded plunger that, in turn, pushes a diaphragm in and out of the valve to control water flow. Sometimes the plunger gets hung up on the spring, or the valve guide becomes worn, causing the diaphragm to bind. On some machines the solenoid (attached to the inlet valves protruding from the back of the machines) can be removed without too much trouble for servicing. Note that on some models the inlet valves and solenoid are made in one piece and cannot be disassembled for servicing.

Dehumidifiers

A dehumidifier, which works very much like an air conditioner, collects and condenses water vapor. If it works efficiently, water will collect in the drip pan beneath the machine. If it stays there without being emptied, the water becomes stagnant and may eventually be reevaporated. And if the dehumidifier keeps running, the pan will fill, then overflow.

Many machines avoid this with some type of sensing system. On older or more basic machines it may be a warning light. On many machines it is an overflow sensing switch that turns off the dehumidifier when the pan is full. Typically, this device has a tube that extends down into the pan. As the water level rises, air trapped in the tube applies increasing pressure on the switch until a preset limit is reached. A faulty switch on a working dehumidifier will quickly produce an overflow.

You may be able to save an appliance service call by cleaning the tube of dust and debris picked up from the pan. You will have to remove the machine's cover (only after disconnecting the power) and screws holding the switch to the chassis to make a thorough inspection. A volt-ohm test meter, connected to the switch leads, should register zero with the switch out of the water, then jump to a higher reading when the switch is lowered into the pan.

JUST ASK

Q What are the pros and cons of using an oil- or water-filled room heater, as opposed to a conventional resistance heater?

A Standard resistance heaters provide heat in noticeable cycles, like a forced hot-air heating system. When the burner and fan are running, the room warms up; when they stop, the room cools and sometimes feels quite chilly just before the thermostat calls for heat again.

Oil- and water-filled heaters provide more uniform heat, like a hot-water baseboard furnace system. They can't heat a room as quickly as a forced hot-air system because the water has to get hot first, then exchange its heat through the pipes and into the air, usually behind baseboard convectors.

This delay as the water heats has a moderating effect on the room temperature because water inside a sealed-pipe system becomes a thermal mass that stores heat, then continues to radiate some heat even after the thermostat has cut the current flow. Room heaters with oil or water are like the tortoise: Temperatures reach 250–300° F with slow but steady heat. Straight resistance heaters are more like the hare: Temperatures reach 400–450° F with heat supplied in more concentrated bursts.

These characteristics make filled heaters a good choice for supplemental room heat and conventional resistance heaters (or even heat lamps) a good choice in bathrooms where extra heat may be needed quickly but for only a few minutes.

For a copy of test results comparing standard and filled electric heaters called *The Reifel Report,* write Intertherm Inc. (a major manufacturer in this field), 10820 Sunset Office Dr., St. Louis, MO 63127.

MARCH

1   INDOOR AIR QUALITY:
Modern Materials May Pose Problems in Tight Houses

Chemical factories discharging deadly gases and cities disappearing in dense smog are highly visible signs of man polluting the atmosphere. And for many city and suburban residents it may not be very pleasant, or healthful, to step outside and take a breath of "fresh" air.

2   FIRE SAFETY IS A DEADLY SERIOUS SUBJECT:
Is Your Home Adequately Protected?

Fuel for a house fire is the house itself—and its contents. The front door, kitchen table, drapes, rugs, and linens burn; many synthetic fabrics and plastics may not burst into flames, but they add lethal smoke and fumes to a fire. Compound these potential hazards with

3   PROTECTING AGAINST PERILS:
Unraveling the Mysteries of Home Insurance

Do you know the answers to these questions about insurance for your apartment, co-op, condominium, or house: Which of the eight forms of insurance do you have? What amount of coverage do you have on the structure and on personal property? What would it cost

4   SAFE AND SOUND:
Getting Your House Ready for a Vacation

If you're planning to stop the paper delivery, pull down the shades and close the curtains, turn off all the lights, and lock away the rakes, wheelbarrow, and garden hose in the garage, why not leave a big sign on the front door instead? "Dear Burglar: We're on vacation, so help

Home Safety

But what about inside? According to the American Lung Association, the average American is inside 90 percent of the time, more than half that time at home.

burning cigarettes, matches, candles, and other intermittent flame sources and it's surprising that home-fire statistics are not even more grizzly.

to rebuild or refurnish after a fire, and are you covered for 80 percent of those costs? The answers are important, because one of the endless catastrophes listed in actuarial tables just might happen to your home.

yourself." There are two ways to stop burglars: with hardware and with camouflage. A sensible combination can make an effective defense.

1

INDOOR AIR QUALITY

Modern Materials May Pose Problems in Tight Houses

Chemical factories discharging deadly gases and cities disappearing in dense smog are highly visible signs of man polluting the atmosphere. And for many city and suburban residents it may not be very pleasant, or healthful, to step outside and take a breath of "fresh" air. But what about inside? According to the American Lung Association, the average American is inside 90 percent of the time, and more than half that time at home.

When energy was inexpensive (home heating oil cost less than twenty-five cents a gallon through the early seventies), little cracks around windows and doors hardly mattered. I remember trying to impress the first builder I worked for as an apprentice by nailing plywood sheathing on a house with tight-fitting, cabinet-quality joints. "Don't build it like a coffin," he said. "The house has to breathe a little."

Even fifteen years ago that was still good practice: let the house vent excess moisture; encourage air exchange at the minor expense of a few more gallons of fuel oil; build with a sensible margin for swelling and shrinking of materials; build a breathing

Large, well-ventilated indoor spaces are least affected by pollutants, which have the greatest effect in tight, energy-efficient homes.

house. There were fewer sources of interior air pollution then and fewer contaminants trapped inside the house.

Now there are many more contributors to unhealthy, unpleasant air, and more of those contaminants are trapped inside both new, tightly built homes and older homes retrofitted for energy efficiency. The American Lung Association attributes most of the problems to seven pollutants, including what they call self-evident air pollutants such as tobacco smoke and the by-products of aerosol sprays. (The association reports that average households contain forty-five different aerosol products.)

Asbestos. This fibrous, noncombustible, and extremely durable material can be found in many roofing and flooring products, spackling compounds, and insulation. Often it does not pose a threat until wrapping around pipes and furnaces, for example, starts to deteriorate and release fibers into the air. In fact, dangers from this form of asbestos are increasing as consumers become aware of the problem and think, mistakenly, that the insulation should be pulled off, swept up, or vacuumed.

Many contractors make the same mistake, which has prompted

some states to start programs for training and licensing asbestos-removal contractors. Safe removal methods are elaborate, and include soaking the material and containing it in what's called a glove box (basically a big plastic bag) during removal.

Carbon Monoxide. This foul-smelling by-product of combustion has become regulated as an outdoor pollutant coming from vehicle exhaust pipes. Indoors, it is produced by unvented kerosene heaters, tobacco smoke, improperly vented gas appliances, wood stoves, and other sources. Some studies have traced abnormally high levels inside to exhaust from cars started or warmed up in attached garages or just outside the house.

Formaldehyde. Formaldehyde gas seeping from some installations of ureaformaldehyde foam insulation have caused headaches, dizziness, nausea, rashes, eye and throat irritation, and other symptoms. The number of complaints, a few highly publicized cases where people had to move out of their homes, and legislation have all but eliminated the use of this product.

But outgassing from many other sources, including resins in particleboard, plywood paneling, some carpeting and upholstery, can produce potentially harmful levels in tight houses. Local health departments and private testing labs may be equipped to take and analyze indoor air samples. The 3M Company sells a do-it-yourself sampling kit you send back to the 3M labs for analysis.

Of course, these steps help define the problem, not solve it. That can be a complicated and costly process of removing some materials and altering the air-exchange and distribution patterns in your home.

Microbes and Fungi. Although certain viruses and bacteria are a common, even inevitable, component of indoor air, excesses of what is called cultivated pollution include the infamous Legionnaire's disease. Considerably more common problems such as bad odors can usually be traced to stagnant air and water in improperly maintained air conditioners, humidifiers, dehumidifiers, and air-cleaning filters.

A recent investigation of a twenty-five-year-old retrofitted house in St. Paul, conducted by scientists at the Honeywell Inc. Physical Sciences Center, found that the bedroom used by an asthmatic child was a stagnant dead end. Because of its location, normal interior air currents bypassed the room, leaving it virtually unventilated. A new return air duct corrected the problem.

Nitrogen Dioxide. Also a by-product of combustion, dangerous levels of this gas can accumulate from improperly vented and maintained combustion appliances, such as water heaters and clothes dryers, and from fireplaces and wood or coal stoves.

Radon. This radioactive gas is emitted by some soil and rock with trace amounts of radium or uranium. Granite rock is the most common, naturally encountered source of radon gas. But since relatively few homes are constructed on a granite base, radon appears to be a site-specific risk and not as widespread a problem as the man-made pollutants. However, best estimates, including a recent paper in the *New England Journal of Medicine*, attribute 10,000 cancer deaths per year to indoor radon pollution.

Many of the problems encountered by Honeywell scientists in the St. Paul house are typical of older homes retrofitted for energy efficiency. In this case, the retrofit was completed two years ago as part of a study by the Minnesota Department of Energy and Economic Development (DEED). Alterations to the heating, ventilating, and air-conditioning systems reduced energy consumption 50 percent.

However, the occupants started to complain about bad odors and discomfort from stale air. Dr. James Woods, Honeywell scientist in charge of the investigation, found that several pollutants were being trapped by the tight-house improvements. He reports, "The effect is similar to placing a house in a giant plastic bag. A key indicator was the nearly constant formation of condensation on the windows."

Modifications to the house included reducing relative humidity, adding return air ducts, relocating an exterior air intake for the home's air-to-air heat exchanger away from nearby car exhaust, and replacing the kitchen-range hood with an electronic air cleaner.

While the air testing and analysis procedures used were sophisticated, the solutions were straightforward. And the air quality was improved without sacrificing energy efficiency. However, until indoor pollution receives more attention and analysis techniques and equipment filter down to contractors and homeowners, high-energy efficiency will, in most cases, continue to be achieved at the expense of indoor air quality.

For a copy of the Honeywell study of the St. Paul house, write to Honeywell Residential Division, attn.: Mr. Mark Sims, Golden Valley, MN 55404. For details of the 3M Formaldehyde Monitor kit, write 3M Co., N. R. Susuki, OH and SP Division, 3M Center, Bldg. 220-7W-02, St. Paul, MN 55144.

JUST ASK

Q A water-conditioning salesman says my water is hard and that I need a softener. Is there any way to tell if this is true short of having a sample analyzed at a lab?

A The hardness (mineral content) of water can be quantified after laboratory analysis into grains per gallon: from soft water with less than 1 grain per gallon, to very hard water with over 10.5 grains per gallon. But to decide if you should even bother talking to a water-softening firm that will conduct such a detailed analysis, try this simple test.

Add ten drops of liquid detergent to a large glass about two-thirds filled with your tap water. Cover and shake until suds form. If the suds are high and foamy you have relatively soft water. If the suds form a low, flat curd instead of light bubbles, the water is relatively hard. If you're not sure how high soft-water suds can be, try a comparison test, using the same proportions, substituting distilled (mineral-free) water, which is as soft as water can be, instead of your tap water.

The Water Quality Research Council estimates that hard water adds $40 each year to the average household expense of soap and detergent; $60 in plumbing repairs and replacements; $30 in shortened life of linens and clothes; and $25 in extra fuel costs. Remember, though, that mineral-free water tastes like liquid cardboard. It needs at least a touch of mineral seasoning to taste good.

2

FIRE SAFETY IS A DEADLY
SERIOUS SUBJECT

Is Your Home Adequately Protected?

In most homes there are many potential fire starters: pilot lights and other flames in hot-water heaters, kitchen ranges, furnaces, and wood or coal stoves; electrical wiring in walls, exposed extension cords and electrical motors in appliances; flammable liquids such as gasoline stored for lawn mowers and chain saws, caustic cleaners, paint removers, adhesives, and other materials.

Fuel for a house fire is the house itself—and its contents. The front door, kitchen table, drapes, rugs, and linens burn; many synthetic fabrics and plastics may not burst into flames, but they add lethal smoke and fumes to a fire. Compound these potential hazards with burning cigarettes, matches, candles, and other intermittent flame sources and it's surprising that home-fire statistics are not even more grizzly.

Fire safety is a deadly serious subject that too many people avoid with the lame excuse "It won't happen to me." Let's hope so. But if there is a fire, it is not enough to hope for adequate warning time, an alternate escape route, and sensible behavior on the part of the occupants, even though it is the middle of the night and none of them has ever been in a fire before.

A practical program for fire safety has two parts: prevention planning and loss limiting. The first preventive step is to correct obvious fire-starting hazards such as frayed, overloaded, or inadequately fused wiring and old, untuned heating systems. Also, separate easily ignited materials from open flames and sparks. For example, don't store charcoal lighter on a shelf near the stove or paint thinner in a cabinet next to the furnace.

A special check should be made in homes with aluminum wiring. The Consumer Product Safety Commission has attributed many house fires to problems with this material. If switch or outlet cover plates are warm to the touch, disconnect the power supply to those circuits and call an electrician. There is a solution, called pigtailing, that involves joining copper wire leads onto the aluminum cables.

When obvious hazards are removed, the risk of fire is reduced but not eliminated. Since no home can be made fireproof, every

Relining can make old chimneys fire safe. The PermaFlu process pumps a masonry mix around an inflatable form from outside the house.

home should have an early warning system. Smoke and heat detectors may provide the chance to extinguish a fire before it does serious damage, or at least the chance to save irreplaceable possessions. Above all, detectors provide time enough to save the people inside.

Early warning can be given reliably and inexpensively with smoke detectors. There are two types. Photoelectric units react to visible smoke particles that deflect light inside the detector's sensing chamber. Ionization units use a radioactive cell to produce a flow of current in the sensing chamber. When smoke enters, it reduces the current flow, which triggers the alarm.

The word "radioactive" scared consumers away from these units when they first appeared on the market, although the U.S. Nuclear Regulatory Commission has determined the devices are safe for home use. The National Fire Protection Association recommends both photoelectric and ionization detectors and reports there is less danger from the minute radioactive cell than from everyday activities such as watching color television.

There is some variance in response time to different types of fires between the two detectors. Some models solve this question by incorporating both sensing devices into one unit. But the discrepancy pales compared to the difference between having either type of detector or none at all. In 1977, when one-fifth of the nation's residences had smoke detectors, there were 6,135 fire-related deaths. In 1982, when more people occupied more buildings but two-thirds of the residences had smoke detectors, there were 4,940 fire-related deaths.

The detectors you choose should bear the label of a testing lab. They may be powered by the house electrical system with battery backup or by batteries alone.

Detectors should be installed on every level of a home, high on the walls, or on ceilings in centralized, open areas such as hallways, where smoke is most likely to spread from floor to floor. Since most fatal fires occur at night, it is important to locate detectors in halls just outside bedroom doors. These detectors are one of the best buys available to consumers: They are relatively low-cost, very reliable, easy-to-install products that offer, without a doubt, the best chance of surviving a fire.

Other preventive measures include planning what fire departments describe as an alternate means of egress (a second way out of a room), particularly from second-story bedrooms where an approved, portable safety ladder can provide a precarious but lifesaving path to the ground. It is also important to conduct a home fire drill, an escape rehearsal that simulates a worst-case, late-night scenario and may reveal the need for strategically placed flashlights, for example.

The other part of a fire-control plan, loss limiting, has an active and a passive role in fire safety. Active measures include fire-fighting equipment such as new (and expensive) residential sprinkler systems with heat-triggered spray heads connected to home plumbing pipes and relatively inexpensive, portable-canister-type fire extinguishers.

There are three types of extinguishers for household use, labeled A, B, and C: A type for ordinary combustibles such as paper, wood, and fabric; B type for flammable liquids such as gasoline, solvents, and cooking grease; and C type for electrical equipment. Since the last thing you'll have the presence of mind (or the time) to do during a fire is read labels, buy one or more dry chemical extinguishers with combined ABC ratings. They cost more, but they're worth it.

Fire fighters have come up with the acronym "PASS" to illustrate the most effective way to use extinguishers: P, pull the safety pin (it prevents accidental discharge); A, aim at the base of the fire; S, squeeze the handle; S, sweep the spray from side to side at the base of the flames.

Should all else fail, adequate fire insurance can prevent a financial disaster. The key is to match the amount of insurance coverage to the costs of rebuilding. Insurance companies generally require coverage equal to 80 percent of home value (20 percent is allowed for the land and the foundation), specified in a standard section of most policies called the 80 percent coinsurance clause. If this requirement is not met, payments for property, living expenses during rebuilding, and every other type of coverage may be proportionally reduced.

Ask your insurance agent for a full explanation of this crucial clause and be sure to upgrade coverage as the value of your home increases. Many families have most or all of their savings in home equity. A practical program of fire prevention and loss limiting can prevent the house and the equity from going up in smoke.

Write to the National Fire Protection Association (Batterymarch Park, Quincy, MA 02269) for information on a series of fire prevention pamphlets. But don't overlook the most practical and accessible information source—your local fire department. They would rather see you now and offer preventive help (some departments even make free safety surveys in your home) than see you later and help you escape from a burning building.

JUST ASK

Q I live in an old house that is not very energy efficient. I want to install a wood-burning stove, but a mason quoted a price for repairing the chimney that's almost three times what the stove costs. Can you help?

A If an old chimney is structurally unsound, it should be repaired whether you install a stove or not. Some obvious signs of structural decay are tipping or curving in the chimney stack (clearly visible to an unpracticed eye); staircase-pattern cracking across the full width and several courses of brick or block in the chimney; and widespread mortar deterioration causing bricks at several locations to become loose to the touch. (Check with several contractors or an engineer to be sure about this.)

In most old chimneys, some form of fire-safe relining is practical. Two systems are worth an inquiry. The Permaflu method uses an inflatable form that is positioned in the old flue, then surrounded with a relining masonry mix that will withstand temperatures in excess of 2,100° F; when the mix hardens, the tubular form is deflated and removed. Z-Flex is a sectional stainless-steel liner, snaked through old flues (even with a gentle curve or two) for a new, continuous connection from stove to chimney cap; it is recommended for all fuels except coal. Information on both systems is available from Chimney Relining International, Box 4035, Manchester, NH 03108.

3

PROTECTING AGAINST PERILS

Unraveling the Mysteries of Home Insurance

Do you know the answers to these questions about insurance for your apartment, co-op, condominium, or house: Which of the eight forms of insurance do you have? What amount of coverage do you have on the structure and on personal property? What would it cost to rebuild or refurnish after a fire, and are you covered for 80 percent of those costs?

The answers are important, because one of the endless catastrophes (called "perils" in the insurance business) listed in actuarial tables just might happen to your home. Granted, the subject of home insurance can be tedious and confusing. Even some of the "plain language" policies contain mesmerizing feats of hairsplitting to distinguish included and excluded perils.

But of all home insurance options, three subjects seem to cause the most confusion. And they are crucial areas in which a misunderstanding could lead to a financial catastrophe on the heels of a fire or theft, often leaving scars even if the financial loss is recouped.

First is the problem of renter's insurance. Surveys conducted by the Insurance Information Institute indicate that only 35 percent of renters have insurance on personal property. Too many believe incorrectly that if their landlord has insurance they are covered, too. Landlords have insurance on the building, the way a homeowner has insurance on the house structure. Grandfather clocks, couches, paintings, rugs, and other possessions inside the building are not automatically covered.

Suppose you're cooking dinner and start a grease fire that scorches paint on the walls and burns your wooden table. Since you started the fire, you pay to repaint or replace the table. That's only fair. But suppose the damage is caused by a ruptured steam pipe. The landlord's insurance pays for the repainting, but—surprise, surprise—you may have to sue the landlord and prove negligence (documenting an improper maintenance program, for instance) in order to collect for the table.

A renter's policy (known as an HO-4 form in the trade) covers furnishings and personal property if you rent a house or apartment against a stock list of accidents—just about everything except earthquakes, nuclear accidents, and a few other plague-and-pestilence-type perils. You have to read each policy to discover the specific exclusions. Renter's insurance is important because it

The result of a hurricane in Freeport, Texas: extensive damage to a wood-frame home while a steel-frame, aluminum-clad home survived.

provides peace of mind and covers losses even if the landlord is intransigent and forces you to resort to lawsuits to recover damages.

The second major trouble spot involves a tricky proposition called the 80 percent coinsurance clause, a standard term in most policies. If a house is worth $60,000 and insured for $48,000 (80 percent of its full replacement value), the policy pays $1 for every $1 of covered damage up to $48,000. The 80 percent figure is based on the premise that even if a house burns to the ground, there is still value in the land and foundation.

But if a house worth $80,000 is insured for $48,000 (only 60 percent of its value), policy payments are based on a percentage determined by comparing the 60 percent coverage with the 80 percent coinsurance requirement, in this case 75 percent. In other words, if you have only 75 percent of the coinsurance requirement (60 is 75 percent of 80), you only get $.75 for every $1 worth of covered loss from the first dollar on. So if the $80,000 house sustains $48,000 in damages, the policy pays only $36,000; you have to come up with the remaining $12,000. Generally, this reduced percentage payment applies across the board, undermining recovery for personal property and additional living expenses during rebuilding.

The third problem area is the industry's version of income-tax bracket creep, called underinsurance. Real estate is one of the very few long-term investments that has outpaced inflation. Between 1955 and 1975 the price per square foot of new homes rose 159 percent, while inflation was up 136 percent. And since 1975, house prices in some areas of the country have doubled, even tripled. With the average cost of a new home approaching $100,000 and the cost of an existing home hovering around $73,000, chances are good that your house is worth more than it used to be—maybe much more.

But a national survey of homes in different areas and price ranges conducted by Equifax Services Inc. found that 41 percent are underinsured. That means they do not meet the 80 percent coinsurance requirement. Underinsuring is rarely a purposeful attempt to reduce premiums. It's a potentially dangerous condition caused by appreciating real estate values and by rising construction costs required for rebuilding. This double whammy can make a homeowner's policy out-of-date inside a year.

Many insurance companies overcome this problem by writing automatic inflation escalator clauses into policies. This way, even if you or your agent do not correctly estimate appreciation or simply forget to increase coverage, insured value will never lag far behind replacement cost. Of course, the value of added major home improvements will not be covered until you notify the agent or insurance company.

A good agent can explain the differences between policies: from HO-1, called "basic form," which is very limited and not even offered by some companies, to the most popular HO-3, called "special form," which covers all risks on the dwelling and almost all risks on personal property. There are also policies to protect condominium dwellers (HO-6) that account for the peculiarities of owning private and communal property, policies for renters, and more.

An agent can explain the options, but you know best how your household operates. Use that experience to make a list of most likely calamities and ask the agent whether they would be covered or excluded. For instance, if you have a house full of Little Leaguers and a greenhouse full of glass, ask about the inevitable breakage. If you use a computer and work in a home office, ask if the equipment is covered. (You're likely to need a special policy.)

You can't anticipate every stray baseball, much less a bolt of lightning. But the answers to a list of real-life questions can provide a common-sense balance to the confusing technicalities of home insurance.

JUST ASK

Q Is it safe to use wood from the lumberyard that's already treated with wood preservatives and to use those chemicals on old wood in place?

A It depends on what you use and where you use it. While many clear sealers and penetrating wood stains are fine, the Environmental Protection Agency recently issued a restriction on three key chemicals: pentachlorophenol (penta), inorganic arsenicals, and creosote, the dark brown oil that gives telephone poles such an overpowering musky aroma. Together the three account for 97 percent of the wood preservatives used in the country. While the EPA restriction (not a ban) is complex, some of its most important provisions are instructive.

- Sale and use of the three chemicals will be limited to certified applicators.
- Penta products will carry a warning of exposure to women during pregnancy.
- Penta and creosote may not be applied indoors, although your nose would rule out this option if your common sense or the EPA did not.
- Penta and creosote will not be applied to wood intended for use inside except for supports—such as building poles in contact with the soil—used in barns, stables, and similar sites.
- Penta will not be applied to logs used in home construction.
- The chemical producers will begin a program to reduce, then virtually eliminate, dioxin contaminants in penta (to one part per million within eighteen months)

I would be comfortable using treated wood on porches and decks outside the house, without painting or sealing or avoiding barefoot traffic. More details on the EPA restriction are available from an excellent source: National Pesticide Information Clearinghouse, P.O. Drawer 2031, San Benito, TX 78586, 800-858-7378.

SAFE AND SOUND

Getting Your House Ready for a Vacation

I hope you are lucky enough to get away for a vacation some-time soon. And I hope your home isn't robbed while you are away. "Not my home," you say? If you're planning to stop the paper delivery, pull down the shades and close the curtains, turn off all the lights, and lock away the rakes, wheelbarrow, and garden hose in the garage, why not leave a big sign on the front door instead? "Dear Burglar: We're on vacation, so help yourself."

The reason for stopping the newspaper deliveries is so papers don't pile up and advertise the fact that you're away, right? Well, I want the delivery boy at the house every day—he can toss the paper in the garbage can or simply replace the day-old edition with a current one. The point is there are two ways to stop burglars: with hardware (such as dead-bolt door locks and screws connecting the frames of double-hung windows) and with camouflage (which is the slightly sneaky art of making a home look as though it's occupied even when it's empty).

Good security hardware may stop an inexperienced thief but not a professional burglar who has decided the occupants are not

*Powerful lighting, such as GE's quartz lamp, combined with
high-security dead bolts, such as the Medico D10, discourage burglaries.*

home. However, if a burglar casing the neighborhood is convinced
that your home is occupied, he may never get to the hard line of
defense—the locks and bolts.

It's a mistake to hide away the common signs of daily life.
Would you rather lose a rake and a garden hose or the contents
of your home? If there is usually a rake leaning against the
garage, leave it there. Leave some trash in the garbage can. Ask
neighbors to dump some of theirs in while you are away. Get the
leaves raked and grass mowed. Better to have a trusted friend
come in every day to feed the dogs or cats than to board the pets
at a kennel. The more activity the better. Maybe your neighbors
will pull their car into your driveway. Use friends, neighbors, and
your imagination to re-create normal household activity.

There are a few security gadgets that will help if you can't find
someone to house-sit full-time. Inexpensive twenty-four-hour timers plugged into lamps in different parts of the house can be
programmed to simulate your living patterns. For example, liv-
ing-room lights can be set to turn on at dusk and off at bedtime,
when a second timer turns on lights upstairs. These devices are
easy to operate. Plug the timer into a wall outlet and then plug
a lamp or even a radio into the timer. Set the twenty-four-hour dial
to turn the power on and off when you would if you were home.

Outside lights are important, too. If other yards in the neighborhood are generally flooded with light in the evening, yours will stand out if it's dark (or if the lights are on twenty-four hours a day). Since outside floodlights are not plug-in lamps, you have to use a different device. Brookstone Supply (Vose Farm Rd., Peterborough, NH 03458), other mail-order firms, and many electrical-supply stores carry light-sensitive switches. Most simply screw into an outside socket between the fixture and the flood lamp. As daylight fades, the light-sensitive switch completes the connection between fixture and bulb. At daybreak the sensor breaks the circuit, and the floodlight goes off.

Granted, there are more elaborate (and much more expensive) electronic security systems. But many security-conscious consumers who have wired up their homes with sophisticated infrared motion sensors and such wind up disconnecting their systems. Whole-house, hi-tech, electronic security systems are difficult to debug and routinely give out false alarms. After the buzzers and beepers and bells have driven the neighbors crazy (and you've apologized to the police for bringing them out on a false alarm), you may want to pull the plug on the system just to get a little peace and quiet.

It makes sense to tell trusted neighbors you will be away—in fact, ask at the local police department about a national program called Neighborhood Watch, which is an organized version of looking out for your friends—but don't tell anyone else.

Light timers, a phone-answering machine (to prevent a burglar from confirming your absence with repeated unanswered calls), and the appearance of normal day-to-day activity all help to make a home a bad risk for burglars.

Sadly, too many vacationers will leave a collection of clues as clear as a neon "vacancy" sign on a motel. And that's where the burglars will go for the easy pickings.

For more information, contact your local police. Departments in most cities and a growing number of small towns have specially trained crime-prevention units that you can't beat for free, impartial, professional—and streetwise—information on home security. In New York City, for example, an officer will review a home by appointment, offering generic recommendations on locks, lighting, alarms, and more. Ask at your local police department—it's likely that they'd rather help prevent a crime now than solve one later.

JUST ASK

Q I have been offered a great deal on eight-foot lengths of seasoned logs. But since I have never cut firewood before, I'm worried about chain-saw accidents. Any tips?

A Movies like *Texas Chainsaw Massacre* haven't helped, but you need not be worried, only cautious. First, chain-saw manufacturers take safety very seriously and produce comprehensive information on safety equipment and safe operation. Write for their literature.

For big jobs, bypass the pint-sized "toy" chain saws for bigger ones with more horsepower and an 18-inch chain bar. Avoid self-starting, self-choking, self-sharpening gimmicks that are akin to fifteen-position electric car seats—more gadgets to break.

Antivibration features are useful, so your hands and arms don't continue to buzz hours after you stop cutting. But the most important piece of safety equipment is a chain brake, offered on many saws and well worth the extra cost. It stops the chain rotation almost instantly and is activated by a guard positioned just in front of the handle on the body. If your hand slips off the handle, it hits the guard, which activates the brake.

If you slip on wet leaves or the chain binds, transferring a kickback to the handle, your trailing hand, the one on the trigger, is likely to lock in place. Your leading hand, the one on the saw-body handle, is likely to let go and rise up to support your upper body and face or, worse yet, to reach out toward the chain in order to break a forward fall. You may think you won't do it, but it's an instinctive reaction. You can't help it, and you certainly shouldn't risk it.

A well-designed guard should cover the fingers and knuckles of your leading hand so that any abrupt motion away from the handle will activate the brake.

APRIL

1 BUILDERS AND BUYERS WORKING TOGETHER:
Problems Are Inevitable, but Preventive Measures Can Tip the Scales

A few years ago the Department of Housing and Urban Development conducted a study of new homeowners and found that one in five

2 CONFUSED BY ALL THOSE TALL TALES AND TRUISMS?:
Some Well-Known Rules of Thumb Are More Than Just Myths

Whether you're buying, building, doing it yourself, or paying professionals, the most powerful and wide-ranging consumer princi-

3 SELF-CONTRACTING:
Getting into the Business or in over Your Head?

A major home improvement estimated by a general contractor to cost $50,000 could cost as much as $15,000 to $20,000 less when the owner acts as general contractor. The possibility of such savings has enticed many building owners to try self-contracting, which seems a

4 CONSUMER MAGAZINES:
Information from High-Tech to How-To

The spectrum of how-to magazines that deal with the home has become a valuable, entertaining, even indispensable, source of information to more than twenty million readers every month. Each of these has its own style and editorial approach, while all stress practi-

Consumer Information

had a serious disagreement with the builder—so serious that one in fifteen consulted an attorney. For $100,000, the approximate cost of a new house, consumers expect better odds. But they might settle for a bit less to eliminate hassles and confrontations and save days and dollars chasing a landscaper or decorator or builder just to get what they paid for.

ple seems to be Murphy's Law: If something can go wrong, it will. But there are other, more positive consumer truisms. And whether they are old wives' tales, rules of thumb, or some memorable maxim overheard at the lumberyard or hardware store, many offer colorful, nontechnical guidelines for saving time and money, getting better quality, and getting more for your money.

simple matter of organization—bringing together carpenters, plumbers, landscapers, mortgage bankers, inspectors, and other housing professionals. But if it were really that easy to save that much, everyone would do it.

cal advice over beautifully illustrated examples. These minireviews of magazines with a practical bent may help you identify those with the scope and approach that offer the most for you.

1

BUILDERS AND BUYERS WORKING TOGETHER

Problems Are Inevitable, but Preventive Measures Can Tip the Scales

A few years ago the Federal Trade Commission and the Department of Housing and Urban Development conducted a study of new homeowners and found that one in five had a serious disagreement with the builder—so serious that one in fifteen consulted an attorney about taking legal action.

For $100,000, the approximate cost of a new house, consumers expect better odds. Most will pay a premium for special quality and durability. But they would settle for a bit less if it would eliminate hassles, insulate them from harrowing confrontations, and save days and dollars chasing a landscaper or decorator or builder just to get what they paid for.

Even projects sewn up carefully with preliminary meetings, drawings, estimates, and detailed construction contracts often unravel. Problems are inevitable. That doesn't mean you should relax preventive measures, only that you should not expect them to be foolproof.

Consumers may grumble about little flecks in the wall paint or a kitchen-cabinet drawer that sticks, but they are generally willing to live with soft spots in a job of reasonable overall quality. More difficult problems often arise from misunderstandings between client and contractor. These are best handled by more explicit construction drawings and a detailed specification sheet listing every type of window and paint and doorknob in unmistakable detail.

That leaves the hard-core grievances: lost funds paid for products not delivered or services not rendered and uncompleted work in general, paid for or not. Be warned: There is no easy answer to these problems. They seem irreconcilable, tempting too many consumer advisers to give desperate clients an expedient and empty solution: Take the contractor to court.

Bad news first. While a popular TV show about small claims court shows how a judge can discover who is right and who is wrong by asking a few telling questions, most consumers I hear from find reality quite different. They may go to court expecting vindication, a cash award, and a verbal browbeating for the contractor, but they come away disappointed and disillusioned. They report inconclusive decisions based on the contractor's baffling explanations of delays and lack of materials, all heard out of context by a judge or referee eyeing the clock and the number of cases left on the docket. Moral: Beware of legal advice from someone who won't be your lawyer, pay your legal fees, or cover for you at work while you're in court.

Builders missing their completion dates, a common problem for home buyers, is minimized on prefab homes such as this Deck House model.

Now the good news. There are several preventive measures short of legal action that offer protection against all but the mot intransigent home professionals. And if you make the mistake of hiring one of the bad apples, these measures still offer financial protection.

Progress Reports. Early diagnosis can minimize difficulties, as it can in medicine. Accordingly, construction contracts should mandate periodic meetings on job progress. Informal, ongoing conversations are no substitute for an official sit-down meeting every Friday afternoon during which owner and contractor (and architect or other involved professional) review a week of work. A fifteen-minute agenda of payments due, materials on order, and such can uncover molehills before they become mountains.

Work-Stoppage Clause. On large projects, ask an attorney about a contract clause that defines when a delay becomes a stoppage, permitting you to use construction funds to hire a second contractor (after legal notification) without financial liability to the first.

Binding Arbitration. It's difficult, sometimes embarrassing, to lay out mechanisms that anticipate catastrophe at the start of a job, when it's important for everyone involved to have a positive and cooperative attitude. But a provision for binding arbitration (by the architect or predetermined third party) will ensure that the job is resolved one way or the other. The Better Business Bureau and the American Arbitration Association both run well-established and successful dispute-settling programs.

End-Weighted Payments. Even small jobs under $1,000 should be paid for in stages: as little as possible up front (15 percent or less) and as much as possible at the end (at least 15 percent). End-weighted payments favor consumers and require bargaining at contract time to overcome the contractor's reluctance. You might not come to an agreement, but it's worth a try. An example: Payments for a $25,000 addition might be $3,750 on delivery of materials, $6,250 on a completed shell, $6,250 on mechanical systems, $5,000 on interior finishing, and $3,750 after the checklist of little fixes and touch-ups is completed. End-weighting would reproportion the first and last payments: 10 percent ($2,500) up front and 20 percent ($5,000) at the end.

I don't favor another highly touted option, a penalty-bonus clause, which rewards contractors for finishing either on time or ahead of schedule and assesses penalties (usually deducted from the final payment) for lateness. While it seems to wield an aggressive financial carrot, it just doesn't make sense. Rewards for speed conflict with the time and quality demands. Also, as late days and financial penalties pile up, the contractor will reach a point where it literally will not pay to continue.

Some professionals may take offense, but reputable, qualified contractors should not object to preventive measures.

Pamphlets outlining arbitration services are available from the Council of Better Business Bureaus, 1150 17th St. NW, Washington, DC 20036 (and from local bureaus) and the American Arbitration Association, 140 W. 51st St., New York, NY 10020. For information on construction contracts and preprinted forms covering a variety of jobs, contact the American Institute of Architects, 1735 New York Ave. NW, Washington, DC 20006.

JUST ASK

Q Is there some limit on closing costs, and how can I know how much they will be? I have heard so many reports of "surprise" costs at the closing that I am worried that there won't be enough money left to cover them.

A There is no limit because there are so many possible charges, from small amounts for paper recording and processing fees to large amounts, for example, 750 gallons of fuel oil left in the tank at $1.00 per gallon.

You are entitled to know what the costs will be before the closing. The best plan is to go over the extensive list of potential closing costs with your attorney well before the closing. Since unexpected costs can literally break a budget, it's important to have enough lead time to gather the required funds. Also, work with your real estate agent and attorney to eliminate any surprise charges not included in the price of the property. For example, it may turn out that the "built-in" cabinets you assumed were part of the living room are removable bookcases according to the owner, who will leave them in place but only for a price.

Generally, the "surprises" fall into two categories: stockpile costs and takeover costs. Takeover costs include built-in furnishings, major appliances, wood stoves, and other potentially portable items. If it's not nailed in, glued on, and screwed down, make sure the item is listed in the sales contract, or it may become an extra. Stockpile costs include remaining charges of ongoing projects, for instance, a partially paid snow-removal contract, a lawn-care contract, fuel oil left in the tank, several cords of wood for the stove. And, of course, there is homeowner's insurance, title insurance, attorneys' fees, real estate tax escrow payments, and some fifteen to twenty other possible charges.

2

CONFUSED BY ALL THOSE TALL TALES AND TRUISMS?

Some Well-Known Rules of Thumb Are More Than Just Myths

Whether you're buying, building, doing it yourself, or paying professionals, the most powerful and wide-ranging consumer principle seems to be Murphy's Law: If something can go wrong, it will. It works on new construction, repairs, appliances just out of warranty—you name it.

There are other, more positive consumer truisms. And whether they are old wives' tales, rules of thumb, or some memorable maxim overheard at the lumberyard or hardware store, many offer colorful, nontechnical guidelines for saving time and money, getting better quality, and getting more for your money in general.

Sometimes we catch ourselves operating on one of these principles—stopping to eat where truckers stop because they travel the road and know the best places—even when common sense or experience contradicts the rule.

But some truisms are based in fact. For instance, August or September is the most cost-efficient time to buy a house. This is a specialized offshoot of a more general truism—buying out of

Would you have guessed that the circular saw, a crucial modern construction tool, was invented by Shaker Sister Tabitha Babbitt in 1810?

season saves money—that applies to clothes, travel, and almost every seasonally sensitive industry. The home-buying variation is borne out by statistics from the National Association of Realtors that show a small decline each year in the median price of existing single-family homes during this period. The 3.9 percent price drop in September was attributed again to decreased demand as families either relocated before school started or suspended their search for a new home until spring.

Many consumer rules of thumb only seem true. For example: Don't buy gas when the delivery truck is in the station. I know of no study that has scientifically measured increased debris in automobile filters and carburetors because of "fresh" gas that contains some amount of sludge churned up from the bottom of the station's storage tank by a new delivery. But the same thing happens when home heating oil is delivered. Years of grunge, left at the bottom of a nearly empty tank, are stirred up by a delivery. If pressed, delivery men will generally advise waiting at least ten to fifteen minutes before turning the furnace back on—just enough time to let the grunge sink back to the bottom.

Here are a few more working words of wisdom and some of the reasoning—if not hard proof—behind them.

- *Flake board is an inexpensive but inferior substitute for plywood.* This may have been true for the first generation of flake board (also called composite board because it is made of wood chips). Now, many building codes permit the use of flake board instead of conventional plywood. Questions have been raised about the glue in some flake-board panels contributing to a fire or fumes inside the house. But the two types of panels are considered roughly equal as structural sheathing. Since composites have no wood grain, they are considered a good choice for long shelves and large cabinet doors where the grain bias in solid wood, and even in plywood, is more likely to cause warping. Also, composites are less expensive than plywood sheathing.

- *Only fools pay suggested list price.* Hard facts are difficult to find on this subject. But from small appliances and furnishings to books and clothing, suggested list is commonly an artificial price purposely inflated so that actual retail costs appear to be bargains by comparison. Suggested list price is often 20–25 percent higher than retail in warehouse-type outlets. Apparently, consumers are more likely to buy a product for $25 if it is marked down from $31.25, even if no one ever bought it for the higher price.

- *Fluorescent lighting is more economical than incandescent lighting.* There's no question about this one; fluorescent lighting is four times more efficient. A single 100-watt incandescent bulb provides 1,710 lumens (a measure of illumination) and is 17.1 percent efficient at converting energy to light. A 40-watt fluorescent bulb provides 3,120 lumens and is 78 percent efficient. Although they are expensive, more manufacturers are now producing various configurations of fluorescent bulbs designed to fit into lamps and other lighting fixtures designed for incandescent bulbs.

- *One of the most revolutionary tools, the circular saw, was invented by a woman.* Often dismissed as an apocryphal story, a Shaker woman, Sister Tabitha Babbitt, is credited with inventing the circular saw in 1810 at a Shaker settlement in Massachusetts. According to several Shaker histories, the idea took form as Sister Tabitha watched Shaker brothers using conventional back-and-forth saw strokes in which half the motion is wasted. She made a prototype circular saw blade by installing a notched tin sheet on her spinning wheel.

- *Neighborhood is the most important consideration for home buyers.* Several years ago it used to be. Now, according to surveys of home buyers by the National Association of Homebuilders, energy efficiency is the most crucial concern, rated twice as important as the size of the home and lot and three times as important as the character of a neighborhood.

- *The self-cleaning feature of ovens is a labor-saving but energy-wasting extravagance.* When you pay extra for an additional feature, it must be a little extravagant, right? Self-cleaning ovens heat any caked-on food to such a high temperature that the spills and splatters turn to powder and can be easily wiped away. To do this safely, extra insulation is built into the oven walls. Recent Department of Energy standards-analysis tests have found that this feature actually improves overall cooking efficiency of conventional electric ranges by 3 percent.

- *It doesn't pay to turn thermostats down, because any energy saved is used when the system reheats the cool house.* Reheating a room from 60° F to 68° F causes a longer than normal burn time. But this expense pales next to what you can save by turning the thermostat down for large portions of the day—eight hours at work or eight hours while you sleep, for example. The rule is you save approximately 3 percent of fuel costs per degree of temperature reduction. Go from 68° F to 58° F for only eight hours at night (one-third of the day) and save 1 percent (one-third of the 3 percent rule) per degree of heat reduction—in this case, 10 percent for the 10-degree reduction.

- *Showers are more economical than baths.* That's true. On average, you can take two showers for the hot-water cost of one bath.

- *Soft water saves money.* The terms "soft" and "hard" refer to the mineral content in water. The Water Quality Research Council rates soft water at less than 1 grain per gallon and hard water at 7–10.5 grains per gallon. The council estimates that when hard water is used in a typical household, it costs approximately $40 extra each year in soap and detergent, $60 extra in plumbing repairs and replacements, $30 in shortened life spans for linens and clothes, and $25 in extra fuel costs.

JUST ASK

Q When, if ever, does it make sense to buy a service contract, and do they really offer more protection than a good warranty?

A Service contracts are more like insurance policies. If you believe all the manufacturer's claims, you don't need the contract. If you think the claims are just a sales hype, you do. Some choice.

And as a rule, service contracts are not cost effective. Studies of average life spans for appliances may not accurately predict their demise. But average repair costs over average life spans rarely even approach the cost of service contracts for the same period of time. For example, industry standards that predict a fifteen-year life span for a refrigerator estimate it will require $75 worth of repair. In other words, a thermostat sensor or a set of door-gasket seals may have to be replaced, but the compressor (the expensive heart of the cooling system) is likely to keep chugging along.

Compare that $75 prediction to fifteen years of the Consumer Checkbook's (a Washington-based consumer group) lowest finding for a service contract ($23.95 over fifteen years), about $360, and worse yet, to their highest quote ($45 over fifteen years), about $675, fully nine times the anticipated repair costs.

If the prices don't deter you, the idea of pooling your interest with consumers who have no incentive to maintain their appliances should make you hesitate. If you take reasonably good care of equipment, you'll require fewer service calls, yet pay the same as someone who runs a mower without oil and leaves it out in the rain. In effect, your diligence will be supporting the negligence of other consumers.

In plain language, service contracts are almost always a rotten idea, too often publicized and sold in the guise of extended, warranty-type protection. Of course, if you buy a lemon, you could use a contract. But the solution to that dilemma is not to buy a bigger and better service contract but to avoid manufacturers who stress service contracts instead of warranties that offer extended protection for well-made products.

3

SELF-CONTRACTING

Getting into the Business or in over Your Head?

   A major home improvement estimated by a general contractor to cost $50,000 could cost as much as $15,000 to $20,000 less when the owner acts as general contractor. The possibility of such savings has enticed many building owners to try what's called self-contracting. On the surface, it seems a simple matter of organization—bringing together carpenters, plumbers, landscapers, mortgage bankers, inspectors, and other housing professionals. But if it were really that easy to save that much, everyone would do it.

   Savings can be dramatic. But reports from the Farallones Institute and the Owner Builder Center (hands-on schools that teach a variety of building skills) suggest that costs must be cut at every possible opportunity, including, for example, the use of some salvaged materials and do-it-yourself labor, to realize 40 percent savings. Still, even a more realistic estimate of 20 percent savings can be well worth the effort and inevitable hassles of self-contracting.

   How much you save depends on the size of the job, where and

how you buy materials, and, for the purpose of comparison, what a contractor would have charged. For example, it's unlikely that a lumberyard would offer you a discount on a single, small order. But on large orders, say, for a room addition, you might get a modest discount, even if it's a once-in-a-lifetime sale, particularly if there are two or three competing yards in your area.

Yet a contractor who spends $50,000 a year at the yard would receive a discount (greater than any reduction offered to consumers) on every order, big or small. The professional also has the privilege of picking through stacks of lumber for just the right board, ordering special materials, and in many cases, receiving specialized services such as computer-generated time and labor cost estimates supplied by the lumberyard to its clients.

In the end you may not save much money buying your own materials. But you will save cost markups a general contractor adds to every subcontract (e.g., for the plumbing and electrical work) and the labor costs of the general contractor, as well. But will you be able to do what the general contractor does to earn that money?

It's not essential to know how to toenail wall studs or install let-in wind bracing. But some familiarity with framing and carpentry wouldn't hurt. It's not absolutely crucial that you know

Behind the money-saving promise of self-contracting are nitty-gritty questions about placing crucial structural beams and estimating costs.

how to sweat copper pipe joints or run travelers for three-way switches. But it will be difficult to coordinate the efforts of subcontractors unless you know the proper sequence of events. Here are some of the most common pitfalls of self-contracting, too often discovered after the job is under way and the positive, do-it-yourself experience has soured.

- It's too time-consuming. Few first-time self-contractors realize how much time it takes to organize and supervise a construction or renovation project. It requires regular attendance at the job site, for one thing. And when you're not there, you must be on call. What happens when the windows have to be installed but the windows you ordered are out of stock? Is it all right to change manufacturers, style, color, price? Can you decide all that over the phone, while you're at work, where you seem to spend more time doing your general contracting business than company business?
- No one is responsible. Working with a general contractor is like putting all your eggs in one basket. You compare estimates for the project and interview several contractors only once. After that, the nitty-gritty details of the job and all the dealings with subcontractors are left to the general contractor. You make one person responsible for the job. Subcontractors who are responsive to suggestions from the contractor, who gives them several jobs a year, may not be so accommodating with you. If the electrician blames a delay on the carpenter, who blames the plumber, you can get caught in the middle.
- You don't really save money. Estimates of savings generally do not include any costs for the owner's time. Technically, you are saving money by not paying yourself. But isn't your time worth something? A major project may keep you from your regular work or cut your productivity so that it costs you money to save money.
- You didn't know enough. Even if you hire skilled and reputable subcontractors, their excellent but separate pieces of work may not fit together. Evaluating the pieces and the whole— and coordinating their assembly—takes experience. Many general contractors start as carpenters but gather at least some experience in other trades. More important, they have seen many jobs from start to finish, encountered the common problems, and learned to recognize their symptoms. During

framing, for instance, errors in planning can be fundamental and cause problems in successive stages of construction. Organizational skills and availability are no substitute for experience.

If you hire mediocre or, worse yet, unskilled or disreputable subcontractors, you may not recognize some of their sleazy or simply inept efforts until the damage is irretrievable. To detect these problems, you should have some acquaintance with contracting business practice (standard contract provisions, payment schedules, and the like) and be able to recognize inferior workmanship and the substitution of substandard materials.

• You're not cut out to be the boss and the client. Self-contracting confuses traditional owner-builder relationships. As contractor, you must be direct and firm in business dealings with subcontractors. Hard bargaining, even suspended payments, may be required to overcome serious problems. Yet, as the client, you should be cooperative and appreciative of good work, positively reinforcing job progress. Sometimes bad blood from tense business dealings pollutes the positive relationship between owner and worker.

Conversely, nurturing that relationship at the expense of hard-nosed business dealings can decrease job quality and increase job cost. (Shaking hands on a contract is certainly a trusting and friendly gesture but no substitute for a detailed written agreement.) It is possible to handle both relationships successfully. But it's difficult. And for some people it's almost impossible.

JUST ASK

Q Instead of learning about construction as repair and maintenance projects pop up, are there schools that teach building, and do they really work?

A To learn about nitty-gritty repairs and maintenance, you should be able to find local courses—at a YMCA or vocational school. (Many offer adult education courses in the evening.) There are more and more of these practical subjects being offered by colleges, too. Another very practically oriented school is the Owner-Builder Center (160 W. 34 St., New York, NY 10001; 212-736-4909).

To learn about design and construction of buildings and additions, it may be necessary to travel to a full-fledged building school—a place where you actually get to build part or all of a house, whether it's a log cabin, timber-frame saltbox, or superinsulated passive solar contemporary. Look for ads for these schools in magazines covering the field of interest. For instance, check the Log Home Guide (information at 800-345-LOGS) to find out about one of the premier log-building schools (one of a solid half dozen or so): B. Allan Mackie School of Log Building, P.O. Box 1205, Prince George, BC, Canada V2L 4V3. Try *New Shelter, Fine Homebuilding,* and other magazines to find out about schools that teach modern construction stressing energy efficiency, for instance, Cornerstones, 54 Cumberland St., Brunswick, ME 04011. The state department of education is also a good source of information.

CONSUMER MAGAZINES

Information from High-Tech to How-To

The spectrum of how-to magazines that deal with the home has become a valuable, entertaining, and indispensable source of information to more than twenty million readers every month. Reading each magazine cover to cover would be a full-time job, but it's not really necessary, since several address the same general subject areas.

Each of these has its own style and editorial approach. Unlike the various shelter magazines—their range is broad and extends from the mass-market *Better Homes & Gardens* to "upscale" magazines like *Metropolitan Home, House & Garden*—these publications stress practical advice over beautifully illustrated examples. These minireviews of magazines with a practical bent may help you identify those with the scope and approach that make the most sense for you.

Changing Times, 1729 H St. NW, Washington, DC 20006 ($15 per year; $21 newsstand). This magazine has changed in the last few years, expanding coverage from dry financial information to its application by average consumers. Personal financial planning,

New High Performance Wood Filler by
Minwax simplifies even major restoration
jobs, such as rebuilding a rotted window
sill. Super durable, the filler moves with the
natural expansion and contraction of the wood,
and won't crack, shrink, split or fall out.

*For many projects, such as repairing a windowsill, how-to photos
and captions in a how-to magazine can provide just the right kind of
help.*

taxes, real estate, retirement planning, and insurance—both
home and personal—receive regular attention. The magazine's
front-of-the-book news features are excellent—diverse and off-
beat new-product reviews, updates on consumer law, trends, surveys, and more—all crisp and worth reading.

Consumer Reports, 256 Washington St., Mount Vernon, NY
10553 ($16 per year; $21 newsstand). *Consumer Reports* now
offers several special publications, although the mainstay (with

over 2½ million circulation) is the magazine that many consumers look to for in-depth reviews and ratings before buying all kinds of products. Facts, figures, and sometimes nothing more than dry statistics tell the story, leaving taste and style to readers.

Consumer Research, 517 2nd St. NE, Washington, DC 20002 ($18 per year; $24 newsstand). This publication, one of the "other" consumer magazines, started in 1927. The subtitle reads, "Analyzing Products, Services and Consumer Issues," which accurately describes the approach. There are no elaborate field tests and rating systems; just no-nonsense, in-depth reports. Without advertisements (the magazine is nonprofit) and only few drawings, the format presents text and more text; it may lack pizzazz but not useful information.

Country Journal, Box 870, Manchester Center, VA 05255 ($16.95 per year; $23.40 newsstand). This elegant magazine has rich color pictures on good paper—a visual treat. Stories are straightforward, written in a very readable, conversational style, and concentrate on homestead subjects, particularly gardening. Most other features are closely related to country living, such as a very thorough article on chain-saw safety in a recent issue.

Fine Homebuilding, Box 355, Newton, CT 06470 ($16 per year; $21 newsstand). The only problem with this magazine is that it does not appear more frequently. "Fine" is the key word: Oversized format, slick paper for elegant color photos, and wide coverage of quality construction are combined with detailed pieces on building skills and specific projects. A nice blend of traditional and innovative subject matter.

Fine Woodworking. Box 355, Newtown, CT 06470 ($16 per year for six issues; $21 newsstand). Taunton Press's sister publication to *Fine Homebuilding*, with the same format, style, and quality. But whereas the building magazine is interesting and useful for both amateurs and professionals, many of the stories in this woodworking magazine assume a moderate to high degree of reader proficiency, as well as assuming that readers have a reasonably elaborate shop.

Family Handyman, 1999 Shepard Rd., St Paul, MN 55116 ($9.95 per year for ten issues; $17.50 newsstand). Rescued by a new publisher a few years ago, the magazine has been modernized; the layouts are more graphic and printed on a better quality of paper, while coverage has evolved from the home shop to include more general home repair and improvement topics. The approach is hands-on, very nitty-gritty, although many of the projects are retreads of humdrum home-improvement topics from years past.

Harrowsmith, 7 Queen Victoria Rd., Camden East, Ontario, Canada K0K 1J0 ($15 per year for six issues; $18 newsstand). This Canadian bimonthly includes some stories of local interest not geared to foreign readers. (That's us.) The mainstay is gardening, with regular feature stories on energy-efficient and solar design, as well as fascinating case-history articles on wildlife and the environment—all with great color photos.

Home Mechanix, 1515 Broadway, New York, NY 10036 ($11.94 per year; $18 newsstand). It's a bit too early to tell where this magazine will wind up. The first issue in 1985 brought a name change from *Mechanix Illustrated* (the perennial number three to *Popular Mechanics* and *Popular Science*) to *Home Mechanix,* along with more color photographs, splashier layouts, and the departmentalized format used by the competition. For now, coverage still includes home and auto topics with many how-to projects. The word is that *Home Mechanix* will emphasize more high-tech stories and articles on home management favored over nitty-gritty how-to subjects.

The Homeowner, 3 Park Ave., New York, NY 10016 ($15 per year for ten issues; $15 newsstand). Progressing slowly from a bimonthly to a monthly (almost) under new ownership, this magazine has steadily improved its artwork and detail in covering home repairs and improvements, the yard and garden, energy subjects, handcrafts, and more. The scope is very broad, the approach always hands-on and practical.

Log Home Guide, Gardenvale, Quebec, Canada L9X 1B0 ($18 per year for four issues, including winter directory; $18.25 newsstand). This magazine covers every aspect of log-home design and construction, including prefabricated kits and handcrafted buildings, energy code regulations, and new products. It may prove to be the prototype for other specialty magazines on, for example, timber framing or solar construction, where a small readership of ten thousand to twenty thousand can grow surprisingly fast to several hundred thousand.

The Mother Earth News, Box 70, Hendersonville, NC 28791 ($18 per year for six issues; $18 newsstand). Rural self-sufficiency is the theme, with energy-related stories focusing more on stories such as the use of home hydroplants over conventional furnaces. The general home subjects are geared more for homesteads than suburban homes. Regular coverage includes food, gardening, a few projects, practical pieces (e.g., homemade saddle soap), and always one or two weird but wonderful stories like "Build Your Own Hamdolin," an elegant mandolin with wing-nut turners and a sound box made from a ham can.

New Shelter, 33 E. Minor St. Emmaus, PA 18049 ($7 per year for nine issues; $13.50 newsstand). Appropriate technology is the focus, applying do-it-yourself skills and available materials to various home-related problems. Energy efficiency and peaceful coexistence with the environment are emphasized. Its in-depth, comparative product reviews are valuable. But the number of full-page, get-rich-quick ads ("Florida Millionaire Wants to Share Wealth") in this earnest, no-nonsense magazine is puzzling.

Popular Mechanics, 224 W. 57 St., New York, NY 10019 ($11.97 per year; $18 newsstand). Only a few years ago this magazine and *Popular Science* were routinely mentioned in the same breath. They seemed almost interchangeable. *Popular Mechanics* has stayed with its traditional coverage: how-to, plan- and project-oriented pieces on home subjects (although some of the shop projects are a bit old hat), with a dash of science and technology done up in a gee-whiz style. Subject areas also include gardening and other outdoor activities, boats, and probably the best illustrated, most comprehensive car repair and maintenance information available.

Popular Science, 380 Madison Ave., New York, NY 10017 ($13.94 per year; $21 newsstand). In the last decade science stories have replaced some of the traditional how-to topics. *Popular Science* now seems targeted for the computer generation of high-tech users and consumers. Still, there are endless departments and regular features covering just about every how-to field.

JUST ASK

Q I have often thought of branching out from my basement shop into a part-time contracting business and have seen ads for a roof-coating, franchise-type business requiring less than $1,000 to get started. How should I check up on the firm and the process?

A First, be cautious of any waterproof-coating system. The "proof" part of waterproof is often an optimistic description of some "renewing" process that may do no more than extend the roof's life a few seasons. Try inquiring about the process at the National Association of Home Builders (15th and M streets NW, Washington, DC 20005), at appropriate trade associations (check the library for the *Encyclopedia of Associations*), at your local building-inspection office, or with local contractors. If no one knows what you're talking about, watch out.

Check the company by contacting the Better Business Bureau, your local Chamber of Commerce, the Department of Consumer Protection, even the attorney general's office in the firm's home state. The most obvious red flags are a promise of quick and dramatically high returns on your investment and pressure to recruit your friends and sell them distributorships that make your investment back in spades. In some cases you pay for the right to sell what you just bought, and that's about all.

Business-opportunity schemes that use multilevel selling, a form of pyramiding not unlike a chain-letter operation, make money for people at the top of the pyramid but not for the people at the bottom. Consider that in a pyramid scheme, where each buyer brings in six more buyers, in only nine steps (selling levels of the ever-widening pyramid from one to six to thirty-six, etc.) some ten million distributors would have to be recruited—an unlikely possibility even if the waterproofing system is the best of all possible products.

MAY

1
THE BUILDING SITE:
The Right One Is Hard to Find

Allowing even a one-hour, one-way commute home from the heart of any large city, it is difficult to find an ideal building site at the end of the trip. You may find a nice home in a friendly town, in a good school district, relatively close to stores and theaters, with reasonable

2
PREFAB HOMES:
Cheaper, Better, or Both?

Prefab used to be a dirty word. From the outset, prefabricated homes were thought of as pint-sized, metal-sided cigar boxes propped up on concrete blocks in a trailer park. They were starter homes— expedient, temporary. Home manufacturers long have labored under

3
LOG HOMES REALLY STACK UP:
Today's Elegant Versions Are a Far
Cry from Their Rustic Ancestors

How do you picture a log home? As a rustic one-room cabin at the end of a bumpy dirt road? Or a charming but damp and drafty place with hurricane lamps, extra blankets on the beds, and coats hung on pegs by the door? Log homes have come a long way; for instance they

4
EARTH-SHELTERED HOMES:
Light, Livable Houses Shed the
Basement Image

Spring is the time to think about building, adding on, remodeling; a time to consider all the alternatives including some form of earth sheltering. While the idea of building all or part of a house in the ground evokes images of wet basements on a grand scale, new water-

Home Design Options

taxes and a Little League field. But those are social concerns about the quality of home life and neighborhood; they have little to do with sunlight, air, mildew, foundation cracks, wet basements, and other by-products of the physical building site.

the trailer-park onus. But new flexible designs and manufacturing methods have spawned a new breed of manufactured homes.

can range from an elegant, 2,600-square-foot model with a 22-by-20-foot master bedroom suite, log homes with indoor swimming pools and saunas, multistory resort condominiums built with logs, and all kinds of precut log homes that many owner-builders without construction experience can assemble and finish themselves.

proofing systems prevent this problem, and sheltered sites save energy and money.

THE BUILDING SITE
The Right One Is Hard to Find

Allowing even a one-hour, one-way commute home from the heart of Washington, New York, or any large city, it is difficult to find an ideal building site at the end of the trip. Almost all of the good ones have been used up.

You may find a nice home in a friendly town, in a good school district, relatively close to stores and theaters, with reasonable taxes and a Little League field. But those are social concerns about the quality of home life and neighborhood; they have little to do with sunlight, air, mildew, foundation cracks, wet basements, and other by-products of the physical building site.

From that point of view the best sites are naturally good—gradually carved out by natural forces of wind and rain and natural drainage patterns. The sculpture may take a century to complete. Of course, builders can try to re-create a good site by installing carefully planned drainage trenches, leaving trees to break winter winds, and carting in topsoil and rolls of sod with greenhouse-grown grass already in place. But too often these man-made landscapes, which may work well as independent mini-environments, conflict with the larger environment surrounding them.

Water is the most difficult to control. Soil disturbed during excavation is easily eroded and may recompact enough to cause structural damage as the building settles. With the right landscaping and drains, rain and groundwater may be directed away from the building. But if the individual site interrupts a natural water runoff of the surrounding area, the larger environment can overwhelm the smaller, isolated, site environment. Sometimes new home buyers don't discover this until the first big storm hits months after they have moved in.

The U.S. Forest Service distinguishes the effects of water and drainage on six basic types of sites. One is a flood plain; low-lying areas adjacent to major waterways subject to flooding during storms, for example, a site near a river at the bottom of a valley. Two is an alluvial plain; areas adjacent to the flood plain formed of soil eroded from the watershed at higher elevations and subject to damage from flash flooding. Three is an upland waterway; similar to a flood-plain site (though less hazardous) where water

An open southern exposure provides light, ventilation, and solar gain in winter, while a stand of trees to the north deflects winter winds.

flowing from higher elevations concentrates. Four is a depression; a site that collects water and where the soil remains wet and spongy for long periods. Five is a hillside; sites that tend to have shallow soil on top of rock and are subject to erosion. Six is a rise; the ideal site with deep, well-drained soil on ridges and gently sloping hillsides.

There are many versions of that ideal building site. But all are at least a bit higher than the surrounding terrain. Almost any natural rise (not the top of the mountain) is good. It may be no more than the crest of one in a series of small hills. This elevation generally offers excellent drainage and virtually no threat of flooding. Although high, steeply sloped sites may provide spectacular views, building on such a site can be costly, requiring special access for trucks delivering materials and elaborate footings to hold the building in place. On a gentle slope of only 8–10 degrees, soil 5 feet deep can move laterally one half inch each year. Special retaining walls may be needed to prevent erosion.

Being higher than the surrounding landscape also makes it easy to get plenty of sunlight and fresh air. That's good for the building to carry away moisture, reduce or prevent mildew, dampness, and rot, lengthen the useful life of most building materials, and reduce maintenance. It's also good for the people inside. Trees along the southern exposures might be cleared to increase the exposure to light and solar-heat gain during winter, while trees to the north (between the house and prevailing winter winds) would be left for protection.

It is usually impossible to visit a potential building site enough times over a long enough period to discover where the sunny and shady areas are and where the snow drifts. But topographical maps, site vegetation, and common sense can reveal much about the environment. For example, a building site on a northern slope will be shielded from winter sunlight, fostering cold and damp conditions during the day. These problems can be solved by selecting a warmer, dryer southern slope.

After viewing a potential building site it is natural to remember a magnificent shade tree or a stand of pines. Also keep an eye out for poison ivy, oak, and sumac, all prolific plants with intricate and tenacious root systems. If a family member has hay fever or other allergies, watch for those plants, too. Information on local vegetation and pollen counts can be obtained from county health departments and from a local branch of the Cooperative Extension Service.

Aside from soil-bearing pressure and other technicalities best left to an architect or engineer, buyers should learn about the environment at the site and then participate in decisions about positioning the building on the site, a process called orientation. Orientation, or how the building is positioned on the site, is also important. But too often this decision is based on convention, simply aligning the building and the property lines or placing the front door perpendicular to the nearest street. Once the entrance is located, the rest of the floor plan may be predetermined—a case of the tail (albeit the "front" tail) wagging the dog. Other concerns may be far more important, for example, orienting the main living area toward the most pleasing view or the kitchen next to a screened porch that replaces an inside dining room during the summer. How you use the house is more important than the symmetry of the site plan.

JUST ASK

Q Instead of nearly doubling the size of our small house with an addition, we were considering buying another small home for vacationing and retirement. Which plan makes the most sense, considering the new tax proposals?

A I'm glad you use the word "proposals." The plan is still a plan, not law. But it has put a damper on second-home buying, even though no one can know for sure the impact of the proposals.

There is a large and powerful constituency for preserving mortgage-interest deductions on primary residences (the construction industry, banks, homeowners, and others). But the same deduction now granted for second homes appears likely to be reduced somewhat if not eliminated. It's an easier target, providing benefits to a much smaller and seemingly more affluent group. While an increase in mortgage interest for your addition will be deductible under the proposals, it's likely that only some of the interest will be deductible on the vacation home.

Another factor in your decision should be the currently deflated mortgage rates, which are hoving closer and closer to the magic 10 percent rate for a thirty-year fixed-rate loan. (The average rate for adjustable mortgages has broken the 10 percent barrier for the first time ever in many lending institutions.) Many mortgage lenders predict that the rate will bottom out at 10.5–11 percent, then head up again next year.

Although the primary-residence deduction is considered unassailable, a recent study conducted by the Harvard-MIT Joint Center for Urban Studies provides a different view. Single-family home buyers were asked this question: "Would you have purchased your home if the interest-rate portion of your monthly mortgage were not deductible?" Of the sample group, 47 percent said definitely yes; 30 percent probably yes; 15 percent probably no; and 8 percent definitely no.

2

PREFAB HOMES
Cheaper, Better, or Both?

Prefab used to be a dirty word. From the outset, prefabricated homes were thought of as pint-sized, metal-sided cigar boxes propped up on concrete blocks in a trailer park. They were starter homes—expedient, temporary.

Home manufacturers long have labored under the trailer-park onus and tried to dispel that image with a string of euphemisms for the dreaded phrase "mobile home." "Prefabbed," "manufactured," "factory built," "panelized," and "site delivered" are current favorites, although no one has yet coined a description with the same transfiguring effect that "previously owned automobile" has on "used car."

Image-altering phrases may have helped, but the real catalyst for prefab sales was financial. As the average price of a new, single-family home mushroomed to almost $100,000 and the escalation of mortgage-interest rates convinced renters to renew apartment leases, builders tried no-frills designs, less expensive building materials, and less of the most costly housing components, construction and labor.

When the motivation is to build cheaper, not necessarily better, consumers can suffer. And substituting materials has caused some well-publicized problems. Aluminum wiring, for example, costs less than copper and has proved to be much more dangerous. But substituting machines for carpenters on some of the most repetitive parts of the construction procedure has saved time and money and finally started to produce an architecturally diverse second generation of prefab homes.

Last year, one in three new single-family houses was prefabricated to some degree. This year, even more will be sold—more than three hundred thousand at current rates. Now there are colonial, traditional, and contemporary prefabs. There are one-room retreats; 5,000-square-foot estate homes; prefab reproductions of classic New England saltboxes with nine-light, double-hung windows; A-frames (as expected); and earth-sheltered dwellings with triple-layer, solar-collecting glazing walls.

Prefab housing isn't homogeneous anymore. Log construction —a vital segment of the industry, with its own specialty magazines and trade associations—is not limited to a series of rustic cabins. Adventurous, precut kits have been exported to Japan. And one company has built a multistory log-wall condominium on the California coast.

New variation in design has been matched by variation in size. Although most firms offer homes from 1,000 to 2,000 square feet, there are many one-room prefabs—16-by-20-foot log, post-and-beam, or panelized buildings with small bath, kitchen counter, and a sleeping loft. For growing families there is a 120-foot-diameter dome, a precut kit with 11,000 square feet on the first floor and headroom for three or four stories above that.

Despite the rehabilitated image and revitalized style, the industry's featured attraction is still a uniformly low cost per foot. Many basic shell kits cost $10 a foot, while enclosed shells (the structural frame plus sheathing, windows, and doors) are $15–$20 per foot. And a few firms offer expansive homes with the best possible materials throughout—imported cabinetry, hand-glazed roofing tile, and select cedar decking. Their costs range to $100 a foot, $200,000–$250,000 without land, excavation, foundation, utility connections, or mechanical systems—your basic half-million-dollar kit home.

But the industry still faces two obstacles: consumers' reluctance to "mail-order" a house and shipping costs. Most firms send a get-acquainted brochure on request, but full-color portfolios of

THE REGENCY

FIRST FLOOR

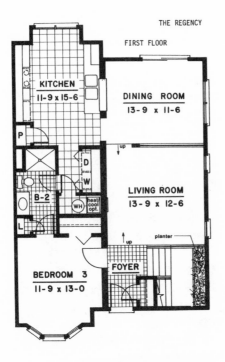

KITCHEN
11-9 x 15-6

DINING ROOM
13-9 x 11-6

P

up

D
W

B-2

heat/
cool
opt.

WH

LIVING ROOM
13-9 x 12-6

L

up

planter

BEDROOM 3
11-9 x 13-0

FOYER

SECOND FLOOR

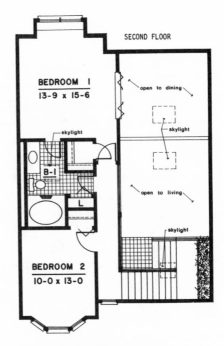

BEDROOM 1
13-9 x 15-6

open to dining

skylight

skylight

B-1

L

open to living

skylight

BEDROOM 2
10-0 x 13-0

THE REGENCY
Copyright: Marley Continental
Homes, 1984

Approx. 1406 sq. ft.

New prefab, precut home packages like the 1400 sq. ft. Regency model from Marley Continental show more materials, more detailing, more style.

plans and elevations generally cost from $5 to $10. A typical package contains twenty-five to fifty standard plans and as much information about the prefab home as you would get from a custom builder of a site-built house. Even firms offering a hundred or more models allow floor-plan alterations and provide a choice of several window styles and exterior sidings, for example. (You don't have to find the perfectly planned house to buy a prefab home suited to your needs.)

Shipping is another matter. Large firms have an advantage here. Although just about every company says it ships anywhere, national manufacturers often have three or four regional plants to reduce transportation costs. (These firms work through dealer networks to provide local builders who are familiar with the prefab systems and are available for face-to-face consultations.)

Prefabs also allow owners to participate in design and construction as much or as little as they want by offering four basic types of packages: a frame-only structural package; a sheathed, closed-in shell; a finished shell, including roofing, siding, windows, doors, and trim; and turnkey homes that are completely finished inside and out.

Prefabs aren't second best anymore. At the very least they can provide competitive, alternative bids that may induce a contractor to improve the price of a stick-built home, the starting date, and the warranty.

For more information: By contacting only two sources, you can uncover most of the prefab firms in the United States; certainly all the large companies. Write to Home Manufacturers Council, in care of the National Association of Home Builders, 15th and M streets NW, Washington, DC 20005; and to Manufactured Housing Institute, 1745 Jefferson Davis Highway, Arlington, VA 22202.

JUST ASK

Q My husband and I would like to have a home built and have seen the house we want in a house-plan periodical. Is it safe to order blueprints from magazines?

A It's safe if you get some information from the supplier before ordering and if you bear in mind that even multipage, detailed blueprints are only a starting point for what will be a complicated, time-consuming project.

Write the company, specify the plan you like, tell them where you will build (the town and county should be enough), and ask them to verify that the plans will conform to state and local building codes. And it's always sensible to make the obligatory checks at the Better Business Bureau and Consumer Protection Agency in the firm's home county.

Finally, contact the building-inspection office where you will build. They should give you a tentative okay, assuming the actual blueprints you order meet their standards. Remember that no matter what the plan company says about the size of timbers or energy-efficiency standards, for example, the building inspector has the final word. In any case, a cordial first visit during which you solicit the inspector's advice can launch a very important relationship on a positive note. Then, if a few details of the plans need to be altered, a cooperative inspector may simply pencil in 2-by-8-inch joists instead of 2-by-6-inch, for example, and grant your building permit.

3

LOG HOMES REALLY STACK UP

Today's Elegant Versions Are a Far Cry from Their Rustic Ancestors

How do you picture a log home? As a rustic one-room cabin at the end of a bumpy dirt road? Or a charming but damp and drafty place with hurricane lamps, extra blankets on the beds, and coats hung on pegs by the door?

Rustic, little log cabins have grown into full-fledged log homes.

In recent issues, the *Log Home Guide* has published stories on an elegant, 2,600-square-foot log house with a 22-by-20-foot master bedroom suite (including bath, walk-in closet, and attached atrium), log homes with indoor swimming pools and saunas, multistory resort condominiums built with logs, and all kinds of precut log homes that many owner-builders without construction experience can assemble and finish themselves.

The range of precut, owner-assembled designs is only one reason for the current interest in log homes. Logs can be shaped in computer-controlled sawmills, sealed with synthetic chinking compounds to keep weather from getting through seams, and treated with a variety of modern chemical preservatives. But the

New log homes, either a precut package from one of some 400 firms or custom-built (interior), are no longer small, drafty, primitive cabins.

pieces still stack up one at a time, not unlike Lincoln Log children's toys.

Building a log home isn't quite that simple. It takes time, patience, some brawn, and a degree of woodcraft that ranges from the most basic carpentry skills on fully precut homes to a fine, albeit heavy-duty, touch with a chain-saw, mallet, and chisel on handcrafted homes. For many buyers, the woodcraft is the most exciting part of the process, and this interest has spawned many schools for log-home buyers and amateur builders. One of the most successful, the B. Allan Mackie School (P.O. Box 1205, Prince George, BC, Canada V2L 4V3) has provided thorough hands-on education for over twelve hundred students.

But most log-home buyers don't have the time or the inclination to build from scratch. Instead, they can choose kits and materials from roughly two hundred established log-home manufacturers. (Some estimates contend that as many as four hundred firms include sawmills and lumberyards that prepare and sell logs piece-meal.) Most of these firms have a unique way of solving the problems of "primitive" log construction without destroying the character of solid wood structures—that character offers contemporary log-home owners a special kinship with resourceful pioneer families that hewed homes out of the forest. Also, kit log homes typically cost one-third less than a conventionally built new home of the same size.

The strength and durability of logs is unquestioned. But many potential buyers, building inspectors, energy-standard and building-code writers, and Housing and Urban Development (HUD) have reservations about the ability of log homes to keep weather out and heat in. In some areas of the country, conventional energy standards, determined by R value (a building material's resistance to temperature transmission), disqualify all but the thickest, fortress-type log construction. Energy conservation is also challenged by the seams between the logs, every 8, 10, or 12 inches around the perimeter of the house.

There are three basic approaches to sealing the joints in log walls. Chinking is a method of mortaring the joints inside and outside. It's very time-consuming but covers gaps and irregular seams so that wall logs do not have to be selected or fitted with great precision. Traditional chinking mixtures combined clay with a straw binder. They had to be rechinked on a regular basis just the way old-fashioned caulking that dried and cracked had to be recaulked.

New chinking mixes are similar to latex and silicone caulks: They adhere well, resist drying and hardening, and have just enough flexibility to adjust to seasonal swelling and shrinking without cracking. Perma-Chink Systems (P.O. Box 2603, Redmond, WA 98052) makes a polymer-based mix modified slightly from a material first used in West Germany twenty years ago as a replacement for stucco. It's applied from a giant-sized baker's squeeze bag—just like decorating a cake.

The most difficult, labor-intensive, but elegant way to seal log wall seams is to scribe, or custom cut, each log (with all its irregular bows and bumps) to nestle onto the log just beneath it. Some builders cut a full-length, inverted-V notch along the bottom of the log so that the outside edges overlap and rest on the log below. Others cut a more traditional Swedish cope (a concave, saucer-shaped cutout) along each log to cradle the timbers together. A scribe-fit, handcrafted log home accommodates twists and knots, different log diameters, and the natural taper of logs from base to tip, and weaves together right-angle corners at the same time. It's as much a piece of sculpture as a piece of construction.

Most home-building firms standardize this fitting process by eliminating log irregularities at the sawmill. Some firms mill every side of the log and fashion some form of tongue-and-groove locking system at the same time. Logs milled on four sides may look more like a stack of lumber than a stack of logs. But uniformity enables owners without the time or skill for custom cutting to fit the pieces together.

Many firms strike a balance between the rugged, pleasing look of naturally round logs and the convenience and weather-tight quality of square-cut, tongue-and-groove joints by milling logs top and bottom only, leaving the visible faces intact.

The biggest question in log-home building continues to be about the energy efficiency of solid wood. The controversy is not caused by the thermal characteristics of wood, a good natural insulator, or by owners complaining of high fuel bills. They don't. It's caused by the R-value rating system used to measure energy efficiency in conventional, stick-framed structures.

Wood has a reasonable R value, varying from about .70 per inch in dense hardwoods such as hickory to nearly 1.4 per inch in softwoods such as white cedar. Using this system, a 6-inch-diameter log would rate R-8 or R-9 at best, while a conventional wall with 3½ inches of fiberglass, plus sheathing, siding, and wallboard, rates about R-14 or R-15.

But recent reports (one from the National Bureau of Standards) confirm an extra energy benefit of solid-wood construction that log-home owners have known all along: logs store heat during the day and gradually release it during the night. This energy bonus is called thermal mass, a characteristic of large timbers not found in stick-built homes and not accounted for in the R-value rating system.

As a result, HUD's minimum standards for wall insulation and whole-house energy performance may prohibit FHA and VA financing for the most traditional American structure, the log home. Only California has written a numerical system for combining thermal-mass factors and conventional R-value ratings into its building code—this despite the fact that the National Bureau of Standards has conducted a seven-month comparative field test and found that a log home used 24 percent less cooling energy than a wood-frame home in summer and 46 percent less during a three-week spring heating period. While HUD studies the question, buyers are showing more interest in the durable, energy-efficient log homes that have been updated with modern mechanical and weatherizing systems but have preserved the rugged simplicity of practical pioneer architecture.

For more information, there are two good starting points among many active trade associations and special-interest publications: Log Home Guide Information Center, Exit 447, Interstate 40, Hartford, TN 37753, 800-345-LOGS, and North American Log Builders Association, P.O. Box 369, Lake Placid, NY 12946.

JUST ASK

Q We have seen a co-op we want to buy, but there seem to be several other interested buyers. Is there any rule of thumb about when to offer the full asking price, when to offer less, and how much less?

A Not that I know of. There are just too many variables; the vacancy rate where you're buying, rate appreciation, neighborhood character, interest rates, whether it's a buyer's or seller's market, and personal questions such as just how badly you want the place and how much of a financial burden you will accept (or should accept) to get it. On these points your personal rule of thumb is the only one that counts.

For some perspective, consider these findings concerning the 1984 co-op and condominium market in New York City prepared by the Corcoran Group, a Manhattan-based real estate firm. In a volatile market where strong demand for housing and very small vacancy rate pushed up prices 20 and 40 percent in less than a year, buyers, on average, were able to negotiate 8.5 percent off the asking price. The average offer was 11.2 percent below the asking price, which shows that buyers fared a bit better than sellers during negotiations. Also, only 12.5 percent of sales were transacted at the original asking price.

4

EARTH-SHELTERED HOMES
Light, Livable Houses Shed the Basement Image

Spring is the time to think about building, adding on, remodeling; a time to consider all the alternatives including some form of earth sheltering. While the idea of building all or part of a house sheltered by the ground seems impossible in the winter when the ground is frozen, it may seem plain crazy as spring approaches and the ground turns to mud.

Many homeowners, all too familiar with the problems of wet basements, might argue against the idea. And to many people the idea of living underground with the subways and septic systems seems like a poor alternative to enjoying the light and air up above ground. In fact, Plato wrote, "Behold! Human beings in an underground den, they see only their own shadows, or the shadows of one another, which the fire throws on the opposite side of the wall." It's not an appealing picture, but it reflects the reservations of many builders and buyers.

While the disadvantages are apparent, common sense and experience can also demonstrate many advantages to sheltering the shelter itself. For example, on hot and humid summer days, the

Most earth-sheltered homes are only partially protected by the earth, with one or more exposures: for light and to increase the sense of space.

part of a building above ground, baking in the sun, can reach saunalike conditions. But downstairs in the basement it may be 15 or even 25 degrees cooler. That's because the walls of the cellar are approximately the same temperature as the earth that surrounds them. And in winter that earth will be warmer (in the northeast much warmer) than the cold air blowing against the outside of the house above ground.

In a report titled "Earth Sheltered Structures" by Lester L. Boyer, reducing heating and cooling loads was found to be the most powerful incentive for earth-sheltered buyers. Other advantages include a great reduction of traditional maintenance. In most designs there is little or no siding to paint (and sand, caulk, and repaint every few years), although in a fully earth-sheltered design you may have the peculiar task of mowing the roof. (Sod is laid over multilayer membrane roofing on fully sheltered buildings.)

As with many recently rediscovered building systems, earth

sheltering is not a new idea. It can be found in some form in virtually every age of architecture all over the world, including "apartments" cut into the sides of a sunken courtyard in China that are two thousand years old. Now there are several styles of earth sheltering to choose from, including only partially buried buildings with windows on two or three sides, elevational buildings nestled into the side of a hill with only one side exposed, and fully sheltered buildings that receive all their light from a large atrium or series of light wells capped with skylights.

As a general rule, energy efficiency increases in proportion to the degree of sheltering. The Underground Space Center at the University of Minnesota conducted a study of fluctuations in temperatures above and below ground in the Minneapolis-St. Paul area and found a seasonal range in air temperature of 130° F (from −30° to 100° F). But at only 8 inches below ground the seasonal temperature swing was limited to 40° F (from 30° to 70° F). At 2 ½ feet below grade the swing range was cut to 33° F. And at 10 ½ feet underground the temperature range was limited to only 18° F (from 40° to 58° F).

Animals that burrow down into the soil for winter hibernation really know what they're doing. In fact, measurements taken 26 feet below ground level (how about a two-story earth-sheltered design?) showed only a 5-degree swing in temperature year round —in an area known for nice summer weather and incredibly cold winters.

Here's how earth sheltering can alter conventional heating and cooling operations. Suppose you are trying to reduce energy costs by turning down the thermostat at night to 50° F. With a typical system the furnace would cycle on and off during the night to maintain even that low 50° F setting; then, when you turned the setting back up to 68° F in the morning, the furnace would fire for a long cycle to raise the temperature from 50° to 68° F. In the earth-sheltered version, the furnace might not cycle on and off during the night because in many areas the soil temperature would be 55° F or higher. (This depends on where you live and how deeply the building is sheltered.) Also, the warmer the building to begin with, the less it will cost to raise the temperature.

Think of heating and cooling loads as a gap between the temperature in the environment (say from 0 to 100° F.) and the temperature needed to maintain comfort inside the house (say, about 70° F). Earth sheltering is a way of dramatically reducing the gap by drastically altering the environment. Obviously, it's more economical to reach 70° F when you start from 50° F than when you start from near freezing.

Here's one instance of how all these numbers translate into dollars and cents. A friend in northern New York State who built an elevational earth-sheltered house (only one front wall exposed) uses three cords (4-by-4-by-8-foot piles) of medium-grade firewood over the winter. And he figures his nonairtight stove runs at roughly 50 percent efficiency. Near the Canadian border, with devastatingly cold air above the roof and a 40° F underground temperature, this limited wood use translates to 360 gallons of oil (at 65 percent efficiency) and about 375 therms of natural gas (figured at 75 percent efficiency).

Certainly, embarking on an earth-sheltered project calls for careful and extensive planning. While the energy numbers are enticing, waterproofing and drainage can be elaborate and require materials and installation methods unfamiliar to both owner-builders and many contractors.

For a wide range of information on earth-sheltered design and construction, contact the Underground Space Center, University of Minnesota, 500 Pillsbury Drive SE, Minneapolis, MN 55455. The center acts as a kind of clearinghouse on earth-shelter information and has produced several excellent books on the subject. For more of a hands-on, owner-builder approach, contact the Earthwood Building School, RR1, Box 105, West Chazy, NY 12992.

JUST ASK

Q Without original blueprints or other records (at least we can't find any), what's the best way to determine the age of a house and its original style? We are interested in restoration but just guessing about appropriate materials.

A You may not have original floor plans and elevations (the house may have been built without plans) but should be able to trace the building's age through records of real estate transactions. Although recording procedures vary, the county clerk's office, or wherever property sales are recorded, is a good starting place.

Uncovering these records can be challenging but rewarding detective work. For example, restorers in San Francisco found that the only complete set of building records to survive the city-wide fire of 1906 was held by the Water Department. Your local building department should have records of any relatively recent alterations to the building.

Uncovering original architectural lines and interior decor will likely be more difficult. You can ask for help at a local preservation society or at one of the firms in the growing fields of authentic restoration and historic preservation. But the best source of information is the building itself.

A handful of experts are able to provide what's called microscopic serial paint analysis. This can show how many layers of paint are in place, the materials used, original color, gloss, and texture, approximate age of each layer, even details of special graining or stenciling. (For referrals, consult the *Old-House Journal Catalog*, published by the Old-House Journal Corp., 69A Seventh Ave., Brooklyn, NY 11217.)

Identifying particular building materials and styles can help. And it's fun. For instance, blunt-ended screws were used widely until 1846 when new machinery made it possible to manufacture self-feeding screws with a pointed tip that are common today. If the old hinges on the old door are secured with blunt-end screws, chances are that the house was built before 1846.

For an interesting booklet along the same lines, called "Nail Chronology as an Aid to Dating Old Buildings" (available for 50 cents), contact the Association for State and Local History, 1315 Eighth Ave. South, Nashville, TN 37203.

JUNE

1 HOW MUCH COOLING POWER DO YOU NEED?:
Follow the Formula

In too many cases a salesperson may help you "discover" exceptional cooling demands that call for a top-of-the-line machine. (What about excess heat from the kitchen stove? Don't you use the oven?) But there is a formula that can provide a straight answer. Known as

2 KEEPING COOL EFFICIENTLY:
Low-Cost Air Conditioners May Cost the Most to Run

When electricity was inexpensive and air conditioners were judged by durability and brand-name recognition instead of by efficiency, the right air conditioner was simply a big air conditioner. But now, when the cost of running the appliance can surpass the purchase price in

3 DOUBLE-GLAZED WINDOWS WORK YEAR ROUND:
Two Panes Make Heating and Cooling More Effective

In Siberia, where winters are so cold that milk is carried home from the store in frozen blocks, most homes have triple-glazed windows.

4 LIVING IN A FISHBOWL IS ALL WET:
What You Should Know about Drying Summer's Damp

Condensation is simply the result of water in the air changing from a vapor to a liquid. It fosters mildew growth, deteriorates paint, rots

Summer Cooling

the WHILE formula, it produces a specific BTU requirement you can match to the rating on an air conditioner for any room in a house or apartment. (Cooling capacity is measured in BTUs, or British thermal units. And every air conditioner has a BTU rating stamped on the manufacturer's plate.)

only a few years, energy efficiency is often the most important consideration.

Three panes of glass enclosing two dead-air spaces is extravagant protection in all but the coldest climates, although many U.S. manufacturers now offer triple-glazed windows. But double glazing is a good investment that pays for itself through reduced heating and cooling costs.

windowsills, ruins insulation, pops tile off bathroom floors, and more. And in a new home (or an energy-retrofitted older home), vapor barriers, storm windows, weather-stripping, and caulking all work to keep the expensive, conditioned air and all the moisture inside the house—a negative by-product of building energy-tight homes you probably won't hear about from your utility company's energy auditor.

1

HOW MUCH COOLING POWER DO YOU NEED?

Follow the Formula

If money were no object (I know it is, but just pretend), would you buy a "good" air conditioner, a "better" one, or the "best" one? Would you want the "economy-size" model or the "full-size" version?

Sears, Roebuck and Co. and other retailers have done very well with this type of marketing strategy—appealing to our desire for quality. The "best" air conditioners are sure to be the most expensive models, with the most buttons and switches and the most cooling capacity—much more than you need, in most cases.

And in too many cases a salesperson may help you "discover" exceptional cooling demands that call for a top-of-the-line machine. (What about excess heat from the kitchen stove? Don't you use the oven?) But you don't need a monster air conditioner capable of cooling a roomful of sweaty joggers eating pot roast fresh from the 400-degree oven on the hottest day in ten years.

There is a formula that can end all the nonsense. Known as the WHILE formula, it produces a specific BTU requirement you can match to the rating on an air conditioner for any room in a house or apartment. (Cooling capacity is measured in BTUs, or British thermal units. Every air conditioner has a BTU rating stamped on the manufacturer's plate. If salespeople talk about "tons" of cooling, just remember that one ton of cooling equals 12,000 BTUs.)

The most general rule of thumb is to buy one ton of cooling (12,000 BTUs) per 500 square feet of floor space—but the WHILE formula is more specific. Each letter in the word WHILE stands for one factor used to determine how much cooling is needed in a given area. You substitute numbers, such as the dimensions of the room, for each letter of the word, multiply the factors, then divide the total by 60 to get the number of BTUs an air conditioner should have in order to cool that room. Here's how the WHILE formula works.

"W" stands for width of the room. "H" stands for height of the room (ceiling height). "I" stands for insulation (substitute the number 10 for a well-insulated area, the number 18 for poor insulation or a top-floor apartment directly under a hot roof). "L" stands for length of the room. "E" stands for exposure (substitute the number 16 if the longest wall faces north, 17 if it faces east, 18 if it faces south, and 20 if it faces west). After multiplying the numerical factors, you divide by 60 to get the required BTU capacity of the air conditioner.

Here is an example for a room 15 feet wide with 8-foot-high ceilings, well insulated (factor 10), 20 feet long, with the longest wall having a southern exposure (factor 18).

Multiplying $W \times H \times I \times L \times E$, or $15 \times 8 \times 10 \times 20 \times 18$, I get a subtotal of 432,000; after dividing by 60, the quotient equals 7,200. Thus, for the room in this example, I would look for an air conditioner rated 7,200–7,500 BTUs.

Of course there are exceptions—a full wall of sliding-glass doors flooding the room with sunlight, for example. But the WHILE formula does produce a realistic estimate, a specific number that will keep you in a sensible ballpark no matter what kind of curves the salesperson throws at you.

Buying the right-size air conditioner is half the battle. The real crunch comes when you have to pay the electric bill for all the restful nights when your air-conditioned bedroom was 70 degrees, even though the rest of the house was a sticky and frazzling 90 degrees.

In many areas electricity is the most expensive fuel—sometimes outrageously expensive. And air conditioners use electricity to produce cooling. But some units use a lot more than others. Over the life of the appliance, your electric bill may dwarf the initial purchase price. So it pays you, literally, to buy an efficient

Cooling Load Estimate Form for Room Air Conditioners*

Customer _____ Address _____

Estimated By _____ Date _____ Space to be used for _____

Heat Gain From	Quantity	Night	Day				BTU/hr (Quantity × Factor)
			FACTORS				
			No Shades*	Inside Shades*	Outside Awnings*	(Area × Factor)	
1. WINDOWS, heat gain from direct radiation of the sun. (Total all windows for each exposure, but transfer only one number, representing the largest cooling load, to the right hand column.)							
Northeast	___sq ft	0	60	25	20	___	
East	___sq ft	0	80	40	25	___	
Southeast	___sq ft	0	75	30	20	___ Use	
South	___sq ft	0	75	35	20	___ only	
Southwest	___sq ft	0	110	45	30	___ the	
West	___sq ft	0	150	65	45	___ largest	
Northwest	___sq ft	0	120	50	35	___ load	
North	___sq ft	0	0	0	0		___
			*These factors are for single glass only. For glass block, multiply the above factors by 0.5; for double glass or storm windows, multiply the above factors by 0.8.				
2. WINDOWS, heat gain by conduction (Total for all windows)							
Single glass	___sq ft	14	←——— 14 ———→				___
Double glass or glass block	___sq ft	7	←——— 7 ———→				___
3. WALLS (based on linear feet of wall)			**Light Construction**		**Heavy Construction**		
a. Outside walls North exposure	___ft	20	30		20		___
Other than North exposure	___ft	20	60		30		___
b. Inside walls (between conditioned and unconditioned spaces only)	___ft	30	←——— 30 ———→				___
4. ROOF OR CEILING (Use one only.)							
a. Roof, uninsulated	___sq ft	5	←——— 19 ———→				___
b. Roof, with 1 inch or more insulation	___sq ft	3	←——— 8 ———→				___
c. Ceiling, with occupied space above	___sq ft	3	←——— 3 ———→				___
d. Ceiling, insulated, with attic space above	___sq ft	4	←——— 5 ———→				___
e. Ceiling, uninsulated, with attic above	___sq ft	7	←——— 12 ———→				___
5. FLOOR (Disregard if floor is directly on ground or over basement.)	___sq ft	3	←——— 3 ———→				___
6. DOORS AND ARCHES CONTINUOUSLY OPEN TO UNCONDITIONED SPACE (linear feet of width)	___ft	200	←——— 300 ———→				___
7. SUB-TOTAL	XXXX	XXX	←——— XXX ———→				___
8. GEOGRAPHICAL LOCATION MAP FACTOR			(Item 7) × ___ Factor From Map				___
9. NUMBER OF PEOPLE	___	600	←——— 600 ———→				___
10. LIGHTS AND ELECTRICAL EQUIPMENT IN USE	___watts	3	←——— 3 ———→				___
11. TOTAL COOLING LOAD [BTU/hr to be used for selection of room air conditioner(s)]	XXX	XX	←——— XXX ———→				___

*For more precise determination of heat load, consult ASHRAE Handbook of Fundamentals.

One section of the Cooling Load Estimate Form for Room Air Conditioners used to select a unit with the right capacity for any room.

unit, one that delivers the most cooling for the least amount of electricity—even if you have to pay a little more for it up front.

Decide just how much to pay for increased efficiency (without doing the arithmetic) by checking the "Energy Guide" label. There is a yellow-and-black sticker on every air conditioner that explains annual electrical costs, compares efficiency among several units, and lists a specific EER (energy-efficiency rating) number, which is the BTU rating divided by the wattage rating. The higher the number, the more cooling you'll get for the money.

Using the WHILE formula to gauge cooling capacity and comparing EER labels to learn how efficiently that cooling is produced enables you to single out the right air conditioner and to get your money's worth up front and in the long term. And that makes a lot of home sense.

For more information, contact the Association of Home Appliance Manufacturers (20 N. Wacker Dr., Chicago, IL 60606). They can provide an even more detailed air-conditioner sizing system using the "Cooling Load Estimate Form" as well as additional details on air-conditioning efficiency and help with major home appliances in general.

JUST ASK

Q What types of buildings require the least amount of heating and cooling? We're looking for a second home in the southwest and don't want to pay another utility bill like the one we're stuck with now.

A One of the most sensible choices would be adobe—maybe an updated design that includes glazing walls to enhance the traditional energy-storage system built into the walls. Mud-mixed, air-dried adobes (the individual building blocks) operate on a naturally moderating twelve-hour time delay, giving off stored heat into chilly air at night and cooling warm air during the day.

Although modern adobes include asphalt emulsion for waterproofing, blocks are still set in mortar of the same adobe mix to produce what is called a one-mass wall. It doesn't crack in the staircase pattern common on modern foundations built with two different materials (concrete block set in cement mortar). It seems that elaborate engineering reports on mass-gain energy performance and coefficients of thermal expansion and contraction prove with formulas and statistical studies what indigenous adobe builders knew hundreds, even thousands, of years ago.

Their architecture, which appears primitive next to steel-and-glass skyscrapers, is in fact highly refined, energy-efficient, inexpensive, human-scale construction never more appropriate than it is today. For follow-up information, try the interesting, biannual ($15 per year) magazine covering adobe design and construction called *Earthbuilder*, Box 7460, Old Town Station, Albuquerque, NM 97194.

2

KEEPING COOL EFFICIENTLY
Low-Cost Air Conditioners May Cost the Most to Run

When electricity was inexpensive and air conditioners were judged by durability and brand-name recognition instead of by efficiency, the right air conditioner was simply a big air conditioner. But now, when the cost of running the appliance can surpass the purchase price in only a few years, energy efficiency is often the most important consideration.

Buying the appropriate air conditioner may seem like a complicated business. EERs (Energy-Efficiency Ratings), BTUs (British Thermal Units), and Energy Guide labels showing operating-cost formulas may seem overly complicated. But the numbers are important when even a small difference in efficiency can make a big difference over the full cooling season and an astounding difference over the ten- to fifteen-year life of the appliance.

One crucial number is the Energy-Efficiency Rating (EER), expressed as a Seasonal Energy Efficiency Rating (SEER) on central air systems. It is the ratio of BTUs per hour of cooling to the amount of electricity (in watts) used to produce those cool BTUs. When fewer watts of electricity produce more BTUs of cooling,

Natural ventilation from operating skylights (they can be cranked open) can be used instead of, or to supplement, costly air-conditioning.

efficiency increases. If you are allergic to energy formulas, just remember that the higher the EER number, the more efficient the unit, and the less it will cost to run.

Many utility companies consider units with at least an 8 EER to be efficient, although there is no national guideline or standard. An analysis of central air systems just completed by the Air-Conditioning and Refrigeration Institute shows that 92 percent of all central air-conditioning systems in the United States are rated at or above 7.5 EER. (Half of that group are rated over 8.5 EER.) In 1983, 85 percent were rated at or above 7.5 EER; in 1981, only 58 percent.

Ratings on room air conditioners compiled by the Association of Home Appliance Manufacturers show that the average efficiency of 1983 units was 7.29 EER. The average unit had a capacity of 10,566 BTUs per hour and consumed 1,088 kilowatt-hours over 750 hours of operation. Over the last decade there has been virtually no change in average capacity. But there has been a big improvement in efficiency.

Here's how the seemingly arbitrary efficiency numbers translate into dollars and cents. On a 36,000-BTU central system (a typical size), with a cooling load of 1,500 hours (also typical) and an electric rate of 5 cents per kilowatt-hour, a system with a 7 SEER would cost $386 to operate for the season, while a system with a 9.1 SEER would cost $297, or about 30 percent less.

But you can guess what increases along with the efficiency rating: the purchase price. So you have to think about spending money up front to save money in the long run. Here is a typical case, comparing an existing unit with a new, more efficient unit. And because the older air conditioner will not have an EER rating on the label, the first step is to compute the rating yourself.

1. Taking numbers from the manufacturer's nameplate, divide the BTU capacity by the wattage rating. Let's assume that the EER rating on the older unit is 5.
2. The EER rating for the new unit will be on the Energy Guide label. Many room air conditioners are rated in the 8–10 range. (The highest rating for 1985 is 11.5 for Friedrich model SM10G10, a 9,800-BTU-per-hour-capacity unit.) Let's assume the new unit is rated at 9.
3. To compare EERs, divide 5 (the old EER) by 9 (the new EER), which equals .56. If your electric costs for the season are, for example, $300, the new unit will cost 56 percent of that amount, or $167 (saving $133 per year).

To compare two new units, use the estimated operating cost data on the Energy Guide labels. Or you can repeat step three for each unit to find the cost difference over one season. In the example above, a $500 air conditioner with a 9 EER would pay for itself in energy savings in four years ($133 each year). After that, it's gravy.

The second important step in buying the right air conditioner is to select the proper capacity. Although there are several formulas that can help, this is not only a question of crunching numbers. Many air conditioners become undersized during an unexpectedly hot summer. Removing a shade tree, leaving the blinds open, and using portable fans to pull cool air into a second room are only a few of the possible variables.

Another problem is that sales clerks often overestimate capacity. It is true that if you want a cool living room on an 85-degree day but also on a 105-degree Saturday afternoon when the room is filled with sweaty joggers, you'll need an oversize unit. It is not true that an oversize unit will run more efficiently because it will run less. Short cycles that start and restart the compressor are less efficient than longer, more regular cycles.

The most basic formula is one ton of cooling (12,000-BTU-per-hour capacity) per 500 square feet of floor space. It is the roughest of ballpark figures but valuable as a check against the most outrageous estimates. The Cooling Load Estimate Form (available from the Association of Home Appliance Manufacturers) is even more complicated but potentially more accurate than the WHILE formula. It is included in the association's booklet, "Consumer Selection Guide," which also lists every model of air conditioner, its capacity, and EER rating—essential reading prior to purchase. For more information on the FTC Energy Guide labeling program, contact the Test and Evaluation Branch, Department of Energy, Washington, DC 20585. Ask for publication DOE/CS-0193, Appliance Labeling Fact Sheet.

JUST ASK

Q What's the best way to stop mildew growth? Our basement has no noticeable water leaks, but the dampness is overwhelming. Even on the upper floor the insides of the exterior walls are spotted with mildew.

A The best answer to your letter (and many others on this subject, triggered by hot and humid summer weather) is a combination of repair and preventive maintenance. Mildewed walls should be washed with a solution of one cup household bleach to one gallon of warm water. A vigorous washing with a soft scrub brush may be needed to dislodge stubborn mildew growth. Then, after the wall is dry, prime any remaining stains with pigmented white shellac, followed by a coat of paint with a mildewcide agent included. (This may add $3 or $4 to the cost per gallon.)

To prevent or at least minimize new mildew growth, reduce the amount of moisture inside the house. Install vent fans to exhaust moist air in bathrooms, kitchens, and laundry areas. If wetness persists, an air conditioner or dehumidifier may be needed. Areas subject to mildew growth, for example, closets where clothes are stored, must be open to benefit from this treatment. Where this is impractical, consider changing solid doors for louvers.

3

DOUBLE-GLAZED WINDOWS
WORK YEAR ROUND

Two Panes Make Heating and Cooling More Effective

In Siberia, where winters are so cold that milk is carried home from the store in frozen blocks, most homes have triple-glazed windows. Three panes of glass enclosing two dead-air spaces is extravagant protection in all but the coldest climates, although many U.S. manufacturers now offer triple-glazed windows.

But double glazing is a good investment, for it pays for itself through reduced heating and cooling costs; it also provides more uniform heat by reducing cold spots common around windows. Two panes of glass sandwiching even a thin layer of dead air also cuts noise transmission roughly in half—an important benefit in city apartments and any house where bedroom windows face a noisy street.

There are many configurations of double glazing. Some are more effective and more permanent than others. But every double-glazing system, even a temporary sheet of plastic taped over windows during the coldest months, is a great improvement over a single pane of glass.

Late-night television is cluttered with "buy four, get one free" offers for double-glazed windows. Too often, consumers buy double glazing in this unnecessary package, giving up better-quality wood-framed windows in the process. Granted, wood windows need regular painting, while anodized or vinyl-clad aluminum does not. But wood is an excellent natural insulator, while aluminum can be about as cold inside as out.

Homeowners who buy double-glazed replacement windows may find they have simply shifted the problem of fogging and condensation from the glass to the frame. Without a thermal break (some type of insulating strip) to separate inside and outside surfaces of the frame, the aluminum will "sweat." Also, note that new units often have to be smaller than the windows they replace, because only certain stock sizes are available; the opening may have to be reframed (a process called packing out) to compensate for the smaller window.

Good wooden windows can generally be renewed unless the sills or other major sections are rotted out. They can be repaired, recaulked, and prevented from rattling by resetting the wooden stop molding that guides individual sashes up and down. Triple track with screen, double track, and removable single panel (you

Double glazing builds in a dead-air space between two layers of glass, an insulating buffer zone between inside and outside temperatures.

put them up in the fall and take them down in the spring) all work nearly as effectively as factory-made double-glazed units, which are often referred to by the trade name Thermopane.

Since exterior storms are generally mounted on the window frame, they may enclose several inches of dead air—a thermal buffer zone. Every building material has an R-value rating for resistance to thermal transmission. Fiberglass insulation has an R value of about 3.5 per inch. Some styrene insulation is rated up to R-6.2 per inch. Even an inch of dead air has an R-.92 rating. Four inches of air space provide about the same insulating capacity as an inch of fiberglass.

The key to successful installation of exterior storms is continuous caulking between the storm frame and existing window frame to seal in the dead air. Instead of installing the unit, then caulking the edges of the frame, try applying a continuous bed of silicone caulk on the window frame where the storm frame will rest. Temporarily tack the unit in place with a few nails, then tighten down the frame with screws so that the silicone is squashed underneath and oozes out of the seam. After a few hours, the excess can be peeled away, leaving what amounts to a customized rubber gasket that seals the energy-saving dead-air buffer.

Adding storms inside has advantages on upper-story windows where the quality of an exterior installation (if possible at all) may suffer from nervous workers who are eager to get back down the wobbly extension ladder. The drawback is appearance. Even ⅛-inch-thick clear plastic sheeting in petite frames clipped neatly to the window trim can look a bit gawky and out of place inside the house. Interior glass panels made by window manufacturers to fit into their own units are more presentable and effective.

Another very low cost insulation (generally under $10 per large window) is heat-shrink plastic film. Adhesive tape and Saran Wrap sound like the ultimate in tacky solutions, but 3M is heavily advertising just such a system. I've tried the plastic film on all kinds of windows (and sliding-glass doors) and find the ads to be a reliable representation of the product, with one minor exception.

The thin film is easily applied on double-faced adhesive tape. It does stick. It does stay in place through the winter. It is optically clear. It effectively traps a layer of dead air. Applied neatly, it is not at all obtrusive.

But it does take some experimentation to get the knack of using a hair dryer to shrink the specially made plastic film. Holding the dryer nozzle very close to the plastic (closer than the directions indicate) and at a 45-degree angle seems to work.

A final note on diagnosing leaks in house windows and storm windows: If the inside surface of the interior window is fogging and sweating, the exterior storm window is leaking cold air into the dead-air space. Exterior caulking is the solution. But if the inside surface of the exterior storm window is fogging and sweating, the interior house window is leaking warm air out of the house into the dead-air space. Interior weather-stripping is the solution. Unfortunately, when this weather front occurs inside factory-sealed, double-glazed windows, it indicates that the seal is ruptured; even though the glass is intact, the window is effectively broken.

JUST ASK

Q I'm preparing to pour a concrete patio behind our house. In digging the foundation, I've learned firsthand what a toll the heat takes on me. Is it okay to pour during very hot weather?

A In addition to harming you with sunburn and dehydration, very hot weather can have adverse effects on you and your building materials. A U.S. Department of Housing and Urban Development report notes that hot and humid weather has the worst effect on productivity. The HUD report projects that a worker doing heavy labor under hot conditions may sweat more than two quarts a day, increasing the pulse rate by ten beats per minute, which produces the same physiological stress as a 14° F temperature increase.

In hot and humid weather it's safer and more productive to start work early and to take regular breaks for rest and water. The HUD report notes that it takes two weeks for professionals (much less part-time do-it-yourselfers) to become accustomed to working in a high-heat-and-humidity environment.

The concrete may also develop problems. Without enough water and enough time to harden gradually, concrete strength is greatly reduced. Hot, dry weather poses the risk of dehydrating concrete, and wind increases the problem, accelerating evaporation to such an extent that the concrete surface may start to set even before it can be smoothed. In very hot climates flaked ice or special chemicals may be added at the concrete plant where sprinklers are turned on piles of aggregate (stones that make up 60–80 percent of the mix weight) to reduce mix temperature by 2–5 degrees. The Portland Cement Association does not recommend pouring concrete in temperatures over 90° F.

Pay particular attention to curing—the long-term hardening process during which concrete gains strength. A concrete foundation, for example, gains close to its ultimate strength in twenty-eight days, but 80 percent in the first week and up to 60 percent in the first three days.

If fresh concrete is left exposed to hot, dry, and windy weather, even dense, heavily reinforced, high-strength mixes will not reach half their strength potential. They are almost sure to crack and may even fail when loaded with construction materials.

Curing is nurtured by preventing quick or excessive dehydration. As soon as the surface is hard enough to hold a worker's weight without marring, curing compounds (thin films that seal in moisture) can be applied by spray or roller. On do-it-yourself projects such as a small patio, the concrete can be fogged (sprayed with a fine mist that does not erode the surface) for twenty-four hours. After a day, protect the surface with thin plastic sheeting or one of the proprietary curing films.

4

LIVING IN A FISHBOWL IS ALL WET

What You Should Know about Drying Summer's Damp

Condensation—your home's equivalent of a nagging, stuffy, dripping summer cold—is simply the result of water in the air changing from a vapor to a liquid. It sounds so innocent, but condensation fosters mildew growth, deteriorates paint, rots windowsills, ruins insulation, pops tile off bathroom floors, and more.

If you live in a relatively new home—built after the soaring price of imported crude oil got everybody very interested in saving energy—summer condensation and mildew can be particularly severe.

Old-fashioned homes tend to "breathe." The inevitable little cracks around windows and doors and the lack of foil or plastic vapor barriers over insulation cause the loss of some precious heat in the winter. But in the summer these old houses let out some of the moisture produced by cooking and washing and bathing (7–10 gallons a day in an average household).

In a new home (or an energy-retrofitted older home), vapor barriers, storm windows, weather-stripping, and caulking all work to keep the expensive, conditioned air and all the moisture inside the house—a negative by-product of building energy-tight

While moisture is controlled inside Kohler's wall-inset Environment unit, excess moisture in baths must be vented to minimize maintenance.

homes you probably won't hear about from your utility company's energy auditor.

Here are some practical solutions. You may not need to implement all of them, since condensation, like humidity, is relative. But with summer heat and humidity hitting full force, you'll probably need at least a few of them.

Remove as much moisture as possible at the point of production. This is done most effectively with vent fans installed in baths, kitchens, or laundry areas—anywhere where you use a lot of water.

In houses, thoroughly ventilate attics and crawl spaces. The rule of thumb is 1 square foot of vent per 30 square feet of attic floor. For greatest efficiency, use a combination of plug-type or continuous-strip vents at the eaves (where the roof overhangs the walls of the house) as well as gable end vents (at the end walls of the attic just under the peak of the roof). If you are not able to install a foil or plastic vapor barrier between the living space and the attic space, use 1 square foot of venting at the gable ends per 600 square feet of attic floor space. In crawl spaces beneath the first floor, the rule for venting is 1 square foot per 150 square feet of bare ground, and only 1 square foot of vent per 1,500 square feet of crawl space if the ground is completely covered with a vapor barrier.

If you can stand the electric rates, an air conditioner will help, as will a dehumidifier, which literally pumps water out of the air. But before you go to this extreme, make sure all the dampness is from condensation and not from a leak.

Basement walls, particularly masonry walls completely or partially underground, stay relatively cool in summer, encouraging water vapor to change into liquid form. It is not uncommon to see so much condensation that you mistake it for another chronic problem—leaking basement walls. This simple test will tell you the difference. Thoroughly dry a foot or two of the wall. (A hair dryer works well.) Then securely tape a sheet of tinfoil over the dry patch; be sure to tape all the edges so the wall area behind the foil is tightly sealed. Wait until the next day to inspect the patch. If the surface of the wall facing into the room is wet, you have a condensation problem. But if the wall behind the foil is wet, you have a leak in the wall.

Another troublesome spot for condensation is in the bathroom, on the toilet tank. Standard porcelain tanks can "sweat" twenty-four hours a day, creating puddles of water that break through the grout and tile adhesive, then rot the wood floor underneath. The cold water inside the porcelain and the warm, moist air on the outside act like a warm- and cold-weather front that produces rain. Improving bathroom ventilation will help. If it doesn't help enough, try one of these solutions: First, drain the fixture, then coat the inside of the tank with glycerin. Or you may be able to get a more pronounced insulating effect by applying a ½-inch-thick foam-rubber lining to the inside of the tank with waterproof resin glue.

One last worry. After you get the condensation under control, you may have trouble cleaning mold and mildew off the surfaces that had been damp. For problem areas, try this heavy-duty formula: Scrub with a solution of 3 quarts hot water, 1 quart laundry-type chlorine bleach (to kill the mildew and fungus), 2/3 cup household detergent such as Soilax or Spic 'n' Span, and ½-cup TSP (trisodium phosphate), or its substitute where restricted.

For more information: Get practical help with moisture, mildew, condensation, and the other unpleasant by-products of summer heat and humidity by contacting the Conservation and Renewable Energy Inquiry and Referral Service, Box 8900, Silver Spring, MD 20907; phone 800-523-2929. Ask for their booklet "Moisture and Home Energy Conservation."

JUST ASK

Q I've uncovered a nest of ants or termites in one of the posts supporting the back porch. The trouble is I'm not sure if the little critters are friendly or hostile. There is some damage to the post, but it seems to be more rot than tunneling. Where can I get an impartial diagnosis?

A Aside from calling a pest-control operator (that's what exterminators prefer to be called these days), who does have some stake in the findings, granted, there are several good sources. The USDA Forest Service has many brochures on identifying and dealing with pests. Locally, take advantage of the excellent services offered by the Cooperative Extension Service. (There is a branch in just about every county.) For help locating them and for information on specific pesticide treatments, call the National Appropriate Technology Assistance Service (800-858-7378). They will provide the name, address, and phone number of the Cooperative Extension Service nearest you.

Another excellent service is provided by the National Pest Control Association (8100 Oak St., Dunn Loring, VA 22027). Seal one of the bugs in a pillbox or plastic bag, for example, send it to the NPCA with your name, address, and phone number, and they will identify the bug, then call or write to tell you the results. The NPCA says there is no charge for this exceedingly helpful service.

JULY

1 ZONING REGULATIONS: *Protecting Your Interests and Limiting Your Options*

Over 98 percent of all cities in the country with a population over ten thousand have comprehensive zoning ordinances and building codes that affect what you can build, where you can build it, and how you can use it. This kind of control extends into the suburbs and the

2 INSURING AGAINST HOME PROBLEMS: *Comprehensive Coverage for New Homeowners*

Although a whole house doesn't break the way a washing machine might, problems with homes, even new homes, can include serious

3 NO-MONEY-DOWN REAL ESTATE: *When the Deal Seems Too Good to Be True . . .*

According to a growing number of entrepreneurs, it is possible and very profitable to buy real estate with no down payment. "No money down" is the catchphrase of several best-selling books on the subject and costly real estate seminars that purport to show consumers how

4 REHAB HOUSING: *A Good Bet for First-Time Buyers*

Buildings in need of rehabilitation represent a sizable market of single-family and multifamily homes tapped by surprisingly few buyers. This may be because two highly publicized pictures of the rehabbing process are clearly unrealistic for most people. First is the image country beyond. About 90 percent of the three thousand-odd counties in the country also have some type of zoning control. Naturally, there are differing views on an issue with such wide-ranging impact on not only structural safety but also design, area growth, and neighborhood character.

leakage and water damage, major structural faults, and hazards to health and safety. One answer to these major problems is to purchase an insured warranty on the house itself. One of the biggest companies offering these warranties is the Home Owners Warranty Corp., with 12,000 participating builders and contractors, and over 1,250,000 homes enrolled in 49 states.

to manipulate the market even if they have never bought a house before. But if it was really that easy to get something for nothing, wouldn't everyone do it?

of a gang of obviously amateur workers unenthusiastically gutting some dilapidated town house in some dilapidated neighborhood for the rights to one of the tiny new apartments inside. Second is the image of some bright young couple who, despite or instead of children, jobs, hobbies, or distractions of any kind, are perennially selling a perfect-looking, fixed-up house in a perfect-looking neighborhood for at least twice the purchase price.

1

ZONING REGULATIONS
Protecting Your Interests and Limiting Your Options

Over 98 percent of all cities in the country with a population over ten thousand have comprehensive zoning ordinances and building codes that affect what you can build, where you can build it, and how you can use it. This kind of control extends into the suburbs and the country beyond. About 90 percent of the three thousand-odd counties in the country also have some type of zoning control.

It's not true that your home is, at least figuratively, your castle, immune from the picayune rules, regulations, and red tape rampant in the world outside. And in general that's a good thing. When you invest most of your savings and a lot of your future earnings in a home, it is reassuring to know that no one can open a pickle factory or a slaughterhouse next door. Naturally, there are differing views on an issue with such wide-ranging impact on not only structural safety but also design, area growth, and neighborhood character.

Separating residential, commercial, and industrial areas is a common feature of suburban zoning. Theoretically, this benefits

everyone in the community, increasing property values as undis-
turbed enclaves of homes appreciate in value, increasing the tax
base, which improves services, attracts corporate tenants, and so
on, spiraling ever upward in value.

But in many small cities this idea of separation hasn't worked.
Strictly commercial zones downtown have decayed because they
are left deserted when everyone departs for residential zones in
the evening. Mixed-use zoning, even office, living, and retail space
in the same building, has helped to revitalize many neighborhoods
while making prime real estate more affordable by using it more
completely.

Before buying a home, it is wise to find out about current zoning
and what many towns refer to ominously as the master plan. This
may be a combination of map drawings and written proposals
available for inspection at the planning board or planning commission. (Different names are used in different places.) The plan may
show the next phase of residential or commercial expansion,
where new roads will be built or existing roads connected, where
a landfill will be started, where a new exit ramp will be added to
a nearby highway—all factors that can change a neighborhood.

Sometimes even the master plan is suspended to accommodate
special interests. For example, you may be surprised when a new
development of single-family homes in your one-acre zoning area
(each parcel must be at least one acre) will have only half-acre

*Zoning laws can help
to insure that a
remote, private house,
such as this one
designed by Sarasota
architect Edward
Siebert, stay that
way.*

plots. In order to build more than ten houses on ten acres, for instance, the builder may receive an allowance from the town for roads inside the development, sewer construction, or special drains. If a large development falls into two different zoning areas, the builder may get permission to average lot size.

While it may be difficult to gauge the effects of zoning ordinances on the long-term development of a town, they can have a very concrete effect on plans for adding to an existing building. For example, it is customary for these codes to control not only the overall size of the property but what percentage can be covered by buildings and how the uncovered property can be distributed among front, back, and side yards.

So-called setback regulations must be considered carefully when expanding a home. Many specify a combined minimum allowance for front and back yards and another for side yards. In each case, a minimum percentage may control distribution. For example, the code may specify at least 50 feet of side yards, with a distribution percentage no greater than 80–20. That means the most narrow yard must be at least 20 percent of 50 feet, or 10 feet, which prevents the people next door from adding a garage that eliminates light and ventilation from your bedroom windows, for example.

Inquire about these codes at the local building department. If the building inspector can't help, try the planning board or the town clerk's office. (That's usually where property records are kept.) If you do not have a plot plan for your home (a measured overhead view showing the outline of your building in relation to the property), the town will. They need it for computing real estate taxes. You're entitled to a copy (generally for a small fee).

There are exceptions to these rules, called variances. And each jurisdiction has its own procedure for granting them. Suppose you want to add a carport to the side of your house that will violate the side-yard allowance. You'll need a variance even though it backs up against a stand of trees along the property line and your neighbor would rather have your car there than in the street where it creates a blind spot as he pulls out into traffic.

Typically, you would have to submit several copies of your blueprints (including a detailed plot plan) to an appeals board and present your case at an informal hearing after posting notices of the variance hearing up and down your road. This is done to give your neighbors a chance to voice their objections. In straightforward cases, present the facts yourself. It may be wise to consult a real estate attorney when the variance involves several regulations or when you anticipate objections from adjacent property owners. It is not wise to buy property (say, a small house that will meet your needs only with a two-bedroom addition) based on a verbal promise of a variance, from the owner or real estate agent, for example.

JUST ASK

Q We are adding a 16-by-24-foot addition to the house. I am confident about building it once the foundation is laid. That's my main worry. How do I make sure the addition is square?

A That's a good question that raises an important point. Often, construction and remodeling or repair projects are not that difficult once the boundaries are established. Starting the job and establishing the framework (literally and figuratively) can be the hardest step.

On your addition, the most practical method is triangulation, using the proportions of a right triangle in which one leg equals 3, one leg equals 4, and the hypotenuse connecting the legs equals 5. To transpose this 3-4-5 triangle to a building site, first decide on an appropriate unit of measure. On the addition of a den, that unit might be 5 feet, so that the 3-leg equals 15 feet; the 4-leg, 20 feet; and the hypotenuse, 25 feet. (The larger the unit of measure, the smaller the margin of error.)

Mark either leg on the house wall, then measure the other leg from one end and the hypotenuse from the other end. It's just like using a compass to construct a right triangle in geometry class, except on a larger scale. After the corners of the addition are set, measure the diagonals; they should be equal.

2

INSURING AGAINST HOME PROBLEMS

Comprehensive Coverage for New Homeowners

A report on new homes conducted by the Housing Urban Development Department and the Federal Trade Commission found that one in five new owners had a serious problem with the builder and that one in twenty-five took legal action. One answer to these major problems is to purchase an insured warranty on the house itself. One of the biggest companies offering these warranties is the Home Owners Warranty Corp., with 12,000 participating builders and contractors, and over 1,250,000 homes enrolled in 49 states.

Although a whole house doesn't break the way a washing machine might, problems with homes, even new homes, can include serious leakage and water damage, major structural faults, and hazards to health and safety, among others.

Of course, every project has a few pitfalls. But even when they are minor or cosmetic, it can be difficult to arrange a solution (usually a compromise) between contractor and client. When the problem is more than skin-deep and involves several thousand dollars of repair work, owners already strapped with new house

Third-party home warranty plans (offered by a warranty company through the builder) insure that many potential problems will get fixed.

payments, closing fees, moving costs, and more may find it difficult to chase a contractor through the courts. And in too many cases the resulting settlement simply is not worth the trouble. Therefore, it is comforting to have insurance against problems.

But home warranties seem suspiciously like huge service contracts. They're great if you buy a lemon. But why should you need lemon insurance when the current price of a new home is about $100,000? The answer may not thrill you: You shouldn't need it, but if you can enroll in a plan, you should get it, anyway. The cost of construction (a staggering amount when you include interest over the life of a mortgage) is too much to risk even when the builder comes highly recommended.

The Home Owners Warranty (HOW) program was started by the National Association of Home Builders. The first house was enrolled in August 1974. The plan was based on a nearly identical program in England that, like HOW, offers a ten-year warranty/insurance policy. In May 1981, HOW became independent, forming the Home Owners Warranty Corp., which also owns the HOW Insurance Co. In addition to the ten-year plan offered by the company, there is now a five-year plan that covers remodeling jobs.

From the consumer's point of view, there are many advantages of hiring contractors or remodelers who are members of HOW.

- Many non-HOW builders offer a one-year warranty on new homes. But HOW's ten-year warranty/insurance policy provides a two-year insured warranty on structural defects and all mechanical systems (heating, cooling, plumbing, and electrical). From the third through the tenth year, the policy provides insurance on major structural defects, with a $250 deductible paid by the owner.
- The policy is paid for by the contractor. The cost is based on various criteria, including the size of the project and the previous performance by the contractor. But the cost is relatively low; the average policy for an $80,000 home is only $176. The policy also includes no-cost, third-party dispute settlement. Also, the protection plan can be transferred with the house to a new owner.
- Instead of a verbal promise or a one-line addition to a contract, HOW builders offer a detailed, twenty-three-page warranty-insurance document that spells everything out. The language is very detailed and provides a more thorough and better defined protection to the owner.
- Since the warranty program offered by HOW would collapse if too many of its member contractors were the subject of too many claims, builders who want to become certified by HOW are carefully screened. They supply references from banks, material suppliers, and previous customers. A HOW member must conform to HOW specifications on all projects. The HOW group continues to evaluate members by following up on complaints; builders must also reregister with HOW annually, at which time their performance over the year is evaluated.
- If a builder fails to make repairs mandated by the policy (e.g., fails to shore up a faulty new foundation), HOW hires another contractor to do the work and absorbs all the costs after a $250 deductible. This also applies if the original builder goes out of business or moves.

The HOW Remodeler plan is similar to the policies on new homes except that it runs for five years, with insurance covering major structural defects in the third through fifth years with a $100 deductible.

HOW's continuing evaluation of its members is definitely an

advantage to owners; it is in the interest of HOW to accept compe-
tent builders so that fewer claims are filed. This is particularly
important considering that HOW reports the average major structural defect costs $9,882 to repair.

Certainly the fact that a contractor is a member of HOW is not
a guarantee that his work will be of the highest quality. So it's not
necessarily better to deal with a HOW builder, although the program does carry a kind of endorsement by association from the
Veterans Administration (VA) and Federal Housing Administration (FHA). Both agencies waive certain site inspections on HOW
homes. The FHA also offers "high-ratio" loans on HOW homes,
up to 100 percent of the appraisal value or cost of the house,
whichever is less.

Another vote of confidence is given by the states of New Jersey
and Minnesota. HOW reports that both have passed warranty
laws that require builders to offer a complete warranty similar to
the HOW policy. In New Jersey, HOW builders are exempt from
the state warranty program.

For referrals to HOW builders (they will provide a sample copy
of HOW policy documents) and to obtain brief but informative
booklets titled "The Home Buyer's Guide to HOW" (for new home
buyers) or "Remodeling Without Worry," contact Home Owners
Warranty Corp., 2000 L St. NW, Washington, DC 20036. For more
information, call toll-free 800-225-5469.

JUST ASK

Q Our contractor has prepared plans for the addition we want to build. The measurements are all well and good. But how can we be sure the space is right for our furniture and how we want to use the addition?

A You never can be completely sure until the building is built. And no matter how carefully you plan, there will be at least a few surprises. But it's not uncommon for new homeowners or addition builders to be surprised when rooms that look so spacious on the blueprints seem to shrink after they move in furniture and appliances.

To get a realistic impression of usable space in new homes, additions, and renovations, build yourself a scale model or draw out furniture pieces on the plan. There are several modeling products that may help. For example, Plan-A-Flex Home Designer provides five hundred reusable furniture shapes at $1/4$-inch scale along with a layout grid. The kit includes stylized but realistic symbols for windows, doors, appliances, electrical outlets, and all types of furnishings that can be positioned and repositioned on the layout board. The kit retails for $24.95. For information and ordering, call Procreations Publishing Co. toll-free, 800-245-8779, or write them at 8129 Earhart Blvd., New Orleans, LA 70118.

3

NO-MONEY-DOWN
REAL ESTATE

*When the Deal Seems
Too Good to Be True . . .*

According to a growing number of entrepreneurs, it is possible and very profitable to buy real estate with no down payment. "No money down" is the catchphrase of several best-selling books on the subject and costly real estate seminars that purport to show consumers how to manipulate the market even if they have never bought a house before.

Although there are many variations on this theme, the essential ingredient is convincing the current owner to provide some type of financing. Since the median cost of an existing house (a resale as opposed to a newly built home) is approximately $75,000, considerably more cash than most people are able to accumulate, most of a home's purchase price is usually financed.

Accomplishing this outside the network of banks, savings and loans, and mortgage companies offering a panoply of fixed and highly flexible financing is certainly unorthodox. It's not risky in the sense of losing a financial investment (other than your investment in the seminar); either you can convince the owner, or you can't. But an increasing number of complaints from consumers unable to cash in on cashless real estate investing and reports from professional real estate agents indicate that it is highly unusual for anyone to be able to buy a reasonably attractive piece of real estate at a reasonable price without spending actual dollars.

Only four and five years ago, when mortgage rates approached 20 percent, most homes were unaffordable to most people. There was an incentive for owners to participate in financing. If they didn't, buyers could not qualify for enough conventional financing to purchase the property at anything close to appraised value. So in order to complete the sale, many owners granted a secondary mortgage to the buyer, agreeing to accept less cash up front in lieu of regular payments or a single lump-sum repayment after, say, five years.

This was a risk for owners: Maybe the buyers would not be able to make the payment; maybe they would fall behind in their primary mortgage payments to the bank, and the bank would foreclose. But now when mortgage rates are low by comparison and

Costly "no money down" seminars sell sales techniques: how to find the one buyer who can be convinced that not taking money is a good idea.

it is easier for more people to qualify for more mortgage money, there is little incentive for owners to take any risks. Why should they when, between the buyer's down payment and the buyer's mortgage, their bank can receive a certified check to pay off the mortgage, and they can receive another representing their home equity converted to cash.

This reasoning is borne out by the reduced rate of owner-financed home sales. The National Association of Realtors reports that at its peak in August 1982, when interest rates were high, owner financing of first mortgages accounted for 18 percent of all financed home sales. The most recent figures show a reduction to 5 percent.

"No money down" may be an overly optimistic premise for cram-course seminars that may not promise results but hint broadly at the ease and speed with which average people can accumulate great wealth in real estate. Some of these programs season the rules of real estate with a strong dose of the self-help, ego-boosting doctrines of pop psychology: Identify the kind of life you want to lead; decide on the level of wealth you want.

Some are crass attempts to make money for the person or firm giving the seminar at the expense of those consumers gullible enough to expect something for nothing.

Most real estate professionals agree that it is possible for astute consumers to use the equity in one piece of real estate to purchase another, which can, in turn, produce enough equity to purchase a third, and so on. This process may be called leveraging, pyramiding, compounding, or turning. Unlike the no-money-down plans, however, it takes time, requires regular attention and management, outlays of cash for down payments, upkeep, legal fees, closing costs, and such, and a good working knowledge of local real estate conditions.

A typical, successful sequence might work this way. A homeowner has lived in the same house for ten years and through appreciating value, home improvements, and paying down the mortgage has accumulated $75,000 of equity in a $100,000 house. The homeowner then converts most of that equity (many lenders loan up to 70 percent of equity), about $50,000, to cash. Depending on the homeowner's income and other assets, that cash might cover closing costs and a down payment on a $200,000 two-family house.

Between rent income and tax advantages, that building may pay its own way (enough to cover mortgage principal and interest, real estate taxes, maintenance) or even generate a cash profit every month. In the ideal case where the homeowner has made a shrewd buy of an undervalued property in a prospering neighborhood, rented to scrupulously clean tenants whose checks never bounce, that property may appreciate in value so that in only a few years the equity can be converted to enough cash to buy a third property.

Consumers who report such success stories generally, but not always, have dealt with familiar property, for example, condominiums, if they have bought and sold one or two for themselves and have watched the condominium market develop in their area. The real estate vehicle may be single-family houses, multifamily attached houses, vacation or retirement housing. It doesn't much matter as long as the consumer knows a good one from a bad one.

The National Association of Realtors says that since real estate is such a complex field, the odds are very much against consumers who may have bought one or two homes striking it rich in real estate. Bill Atkinson of the association says, "If consumers aren't sure what amortization means and do not know the ins and outs of depreciation and other tax implications of income-producing real estate, they should think long and hard before venturing into the market on their own."

JUST ASK

Q Is it necessary to have a written home-improvement contract even for a small job that shouldn't take more than two days?

A Yes. It may seem picky or overcautious, but it is a sensible thing to do. And it is not an insult to ask a home-improvement contractor to sign a written agreement. Failure to get it in writing, even for a small job, is such an obvious, fundamental mistake that everyone should know about it and avoid it. But they don't. Too often a homeowner who wouldn't consider giving money to a builder for an addition without a detailed contract will hire someone to fix the roof or add an outlet based on a handshake.

Writing down a verbal agreement forces both parties to clarify their expectations. It uncovers misunderstandings on paper before they are literally set in cement. While a written contract for a new house or major addition is lengthy and complex, a simple, short letter of agreement will do for small jobs.

In its most basic form, to cover the most inconsequential jobs, the letter simply identifies both parties, the job in question, the price, and the method of payment. A more complete letter, including product guarantees, contractor's liability insurance, a detailed listing of materials, and other points, may be more appropriate for larger jobs. No contractor should object to writing down verbal promises. They should be ready to put it all in writing and then shake on the deal.

4

REHAB HOUSING
A Good Bet for First-Time Buyers

Buildings in need of rehabilitation represent a sizable market of singlefamily and multifamily homes tapped by surprisingly few buyers. This may be because two highly publicized pictures of the rehabbing process are clearly unrealistic for most people.

First is the image of a gang of obviously amateur workers unenthusiastically gutting some dilapidated town house in some dilapidated neighborhood for the rights to one of the tiny new apartments inside. Second is the image of some bright young couple who, despite or instead of children, jobs, hobbies, or distractions of any kind, are perennially selling a perfect-looking, fixed-up house in a perfect-looking neighborhood for at least twice the purchase price.

Rehabbing is not necessarily as hard as the first case or as easy as the second. It need not be a monumental project where everything but the structural shell is rebuilt, where the currency is sweat equity instead of dollars, and where hours on the job are matched by hours of cutting red tape of special grants and inspections and agencies overseeing inner-city this and urban-renewal that.

Imaginative compact designs, such as this redwood deck and pool in Brooklyn, can transform the small, narrow yard of a brick row house.

Conversely, it is extremely unusual for home buyers to pick the just slightly seedy house in the about-to-be-up-and-coming area, to make only economical yet highly desirable improvements, and to find a top-dollar buyer after the last coat of paint dries, all while tending to basics such as holding down a job to pay for the building materials, not to mention food.

But there is a lot of room between the highly visible extremes of rehabbing. And the stock of old buildings is diverse. Old houses may become outdated by current standards, lack modern mechanical systems, waste too much energy, or simply look old and frumpy. All that can be fixed. The really important parts of a house, such as the foundation and sills and frame, wear quite well. Often the problems are only skin-deep. But they can be pervasive. And in an economy so predisposed to disposable goods that passing bottle-return laws causes a commotion, homeowners can become overwhelmed with the surface problems (or terminally tired of making repairs) and move on to a newer home.

In fact, a reasonably well built and maintained home should last a century or more. Tests made by the Forest Products Laboratory (a division of the U.S. Department of Agriculture's Forest Service) show that, free of decay or other abnormal environmental factors, wood does not lose strength for well over a hundred years. Tests on timbers from Japanese temples up to thirteen centuries old indicate that shock resistance (the ability to with-

stand sudden loads) is the only structural value significantly reduced after several centuries.

Except for their energy systems, which are generally no match
for modern, more efficient heating and cooling systems, older
homes are often better than new ones; they are built more carefully, with beefier materials, and very likely possess some highly
prized, old-fashioned features such as soundproof plaster walls
and solid wood doors inside and out.

If it were easy to find and fix rehab bargains, the supply would
be long gone. But fresh supplies continue to surface, sometimes
right under the nose of high-powered real estate developers. In
Hoboken, for instance, unassuming, undervalued row houses
with a panoramic view of Manhattan (and only a short commute
away) recently started to change hands and alter the character of
neighborhoods so rapidly that a moratorium on sales was in-
stituted by the city government.

To select good candidates for rehabbing, some special guidelines may be needed that are quite unlike those used by conventional home buyers.

1. Look for homes that need help (as in rehabilitation), not homes
   where everything works. An inspection report on a good rehab
   candidate should reveal many defects.
2. Look for some evidence of rehabbing in the immediate area,
   unless you like the inordinate financial risk that goes with
   being the only person who believes the neighborhood will turn
   around.
3. Research the case histories of at least two recent rehabs in the
   area (purchase price, rehabbing done, approximate new market
   value, rate of appreciation). It will be easier to convince bankers (not known as great risk takers) of a building's potential
   when you can offer some precedent, some hint of a positive
   trend. Mortgage bankers like to be on band wagons, not lead
   them.
4. Look for buildings with cosmetic problems but avoid buildings
   with structural problems. Even serious surface decay is generally easier and less expensive to deal with than more fundamental problems hidden beneath the surface.
5. Look for buildings needing a minimum of major replacements
   (a new furnace, new floor joists). They are a poor investment
   compared to major improvements (a new deck, finished basement). Because a major replacement offers only a working,

albeit new, version of something every buyer expects a building to have in working order anyway, it is difficult to recoup your investment.

6. Look for buildings below area real estate norms—characteristics used to compare homes such as square footage, number of bedrooms and baths, appliances, heating and cooling systems, and other features. Houses that have everything, but much of it broken or outdated, are a disaster. Houses that have less have more potential. A rehab dollar spent on a $500,000 mansion nets less in resale than a dollar spent on a $50,000 building.

But can basic decisions about house and home be that calculating? It depends on your motivation. Is a rehab, like the traditional "handyman's special," your sweat-equity ticket into the housing market or a way to trade up from a "starter" to a newer, larger home, or even the vehicle for becoming a full-time real estate entrepreneur? If the rehab is strictly a ticket to another home, financial concerns are paramount. But the intricate components that determine potential resale value need not overshadow personal likes and dislikes if the objective is simply to find an affordable place to live, where, over time, you can fix the problems and make the changes that turn somebody else's building into your home.

JUST ASK

Q When we bought our house, we thought we could level off the hill in the backyard. We have a narrow, flat section between the house and the retaining wall now. How hard would it be to expand it?

A From the snapshots you included, the hill appears to slope up at about a 30-degree angle. Mowing the grass on it must be an adventure. Moving it, even if you didn't hit too many root systems or a rock ledge, would be practically impossible. Even getting large earth-moving machines behind the house to the hill could be a problem. Then they would have to cut a path for themselves into the slope before reducing the elevation in stages.

Then, to prevent erosion and other serious drainage problems, even a mud slide (all obeying the law of gravity and flowing directly toward the house), extensive drainage and landscape work is necessary. And unless you remove the entire top of the hill, the remaining earth will have to be held in place with a retaining wall. The farther you cut into the hillside, the higher the wall must be. Also, this project would require a substantial area drain at the foot of the hill to prevent flooding.

A more realistic solution may be to terrace the hillside in wide steps of level ground. This way a series of small retaining walls built of treated railroad ties, for example, can be used to prevent erosion and make the property more usable. Also, this project can be tackled in stages.

AUGUST

1 FROM ROUGH TIMBER TO HIGH-TECH FRAMING:
Today's Economical, "Engineered" Construction

A common complaint of homeowners is the amount of repair work required on their new homes. Too often the smooth, freshly painted

2 THE LANGUAGE OF LUMBER:
How to Tell the Board Feet from the Square Feet

For amateur carpenters and inexperienced do-it-yourselfers alike, ordering materials for a project has two potential pitfalls. First, you may get the wrong materials. That can make the job unnecessarily difficult and the finished product needlessly inferior, even unsafe.

3 BUILDING IN WINTER:
Treated Wooden Foundations Make It Possible and Economical

As long ago as 1924, in a study of the construction industry, the federal government recorded a decrease in construction productivity during winter months. Even such simple tasks as hammering a nail are tough in cold weather, which also increases construction costs by

4 STEEL FRAMING:
Out of the Skyscraper and into the House

Unlike wood, it doesn't warp, shrink, or split. Termites and carpenter ants can't chew through it. It's much lighter than masonry and it's easier and faster to assemble the pieces into a shelter. And it won't rot or crumble or burn. What probably sounds like the ultimate an-

Construction

or papered surfaces deteriorate after only one or two heating seasons; the wooden framework beneath those surfaces dries out, twists, warps, pops nailheads out of the wall, and opens seams between drywall panels. Although most housing, like consumer products in general, is sold on appearance, it is the crucial skeleton beneath the skin that holds everything together.

Second, by using the wrong terminology, fumbling with crude drawings, or pantomiming hand signals to describe what you want, you can get the wrong materials and an acute inferiority complex. Not knowing what to ask for makes you dependent on the goodwill of salespeople who may not have the time or patience to decipher your plans. Not knowing can also make you feel very uncomfortable.

at least 5 percent in most regions. One of the most far-reaching improvements in winter building is a wooden foundation system (yes, wood, not masonry). Until recently, it was known as the all-weather wood foundation.

swer to prevent all kinds of home-maintenance and repair problems is steel framing—a residential version of the familiar structural skeletons of bridges and skyscrapers. In this lighter-duty application of metal framing, connections between structural members are crimped or screwed together instead of riveted. The engineering system is similar to wood construction, organizing a system of sticks (whether wood or steel) into a cohesive frame.

1

FROM ROUGH TIMBER TO HIGH-TECH FRAMING

Today's Economical, "Engineered" Construction

A common complaint of homeowners is the amount of repair work required on their new homes. Too often the smooth, freshly painted surfaces deteriorate after only one or two heating seasons; the wooden framework beneath those surfaces dries out, twists, warps, pops nailheads out of the wall, and opens seams between drywall panels.

Most housing, like consumer products in general, is sold on appearance, not substance. Fancy wall coverings, elaborate lighting fixtures, and gadget-laden appliances often take preference over the structure, even though it is the crucial skeleton beneath the skin that holds everything together.

Decades ago, when labor and materials were relatively inexpensive and a 2-by-4 was really a 2-by-4 (now it measures 1½-by-3½ inches), these problems were overcome by following a simple principle: If in doubt, overbuild. Now, the expense of using 2-by-12-inch joists instead of 2-by-8s, for example, makes this principle unrealistic. Even though wood is a renewable resource, the emphasis in current construction is to design engineering systems that can use less wood without sacrificing strength and durability.

This is not a new idea. Just consider the evolution from solid-wood log cabins to timber-frame structures using beams on the scale of 8-by-8 inches and larger to conventional modern framing aptly called stick-built construction. Now, highly engineered wood-framing systems have been developed that deliver more strength from less wood as well as decrease construction time and costs.

One of the most interesting systems, called truss framing, combines the mechanics and cost efficiency of roof trusses (used in 80 percent of new single-family construction) and floor trusses (used in 16 percent of new homes). The truss frame is like a complete cross section of the building, including floor, roof, and connecting wall studs, all in one slice.

The system was developed by the Forest Service of the Department of Agriculture's Forest Products Laboratory in Madison, Wisconsin. Research engineers there wanted to design a system that would eliminate the weak link between the roof and sidewall and resist uplift forces from high winds. But builders seem to be more interested in other characteristics of the system, namely, that it uses less wood than conventional framing and speeds construction time.

Truss frames are one-piece structural cross-sections of a building that can be mass produced and then shipped to the site for assembly.

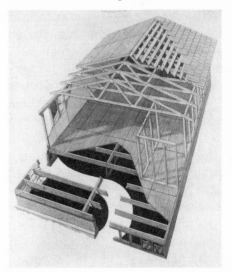

The roof and floor truss sections are made of short 2-by-4 sections called webs, connected in a W pattern with nailing plates. This configuration saves up to 30 percent of the lumber used in conventional framing. And assuming equal field conditions, Forest Products engineers estimate that truss framing offers a five-to-one advantage in construction time. This means that a conventional house framed by a crew of three or four carpenters in a week could be built with truss frames in one eight-hour day.

The lab reports that one Florida firm used a relatively inexperienced six-person crew to frame and completely close in a home (covering the frame with plywood sheathing and installing windows and doors) in one day. A Wisconsin firm, which used truss frames with an engineered foundation system built of pressure-treated wood, took only fifteen days to finish a new house—inside and out.

The truss-frame program is now in what engineers at the Forest Products Laboratory call the technology-transfer stage. After some two thousand truss-frame homes have been built in thirty states and four foreign countries and building codes have been met, engineers at the lab have turned to other projects. Now, they say, it is up to the construction industry to continue development. But there are a few drawbacks.

Truss frames are most economical when they are mass-produced. Since one is a carbon copy of another and an entire setup (every angle and joint) must be changed at the plant to make even a minor design change, truss frames work best in tract-type developments. Also, truss frames work best when designed with low-slope roof pitches. Allowing 20 inches for the floor joist and eight feet for the sidewalls, only a low-slope design can be transported by trucks without exceeding the wide-load limit of 14 feet.

A picture emerges of a truss-frame home as a 1,000–1,500-square-foot rectangle—the ultimate boring little box. That's a picture many home buyers won't accept. But when financial concerns are not allowed to overshadow all others, truss frames can form the basis of some very interesting designs.

Some builders have overcome the wide-load limitation by building truss frames in the shop with two parallel floor trusses, then adding a second floor at the site. Analysts at the National Association of Home Builders (NAHB) Research Foundation report interest in truss frames as the basis of a superinsulated wall in which trusses might be used on the sidewall as well as the floor and roof.

It is true that modifications in the field—e.g., cutting through the frames to install picture windows—hinder the economy of mass production. Builders who deal more directly with housing consumers than research engineers report that many buyers are not ready for the uniformity of a mass-produced system and want to put their personal stamp on the biggest investment of their lives.

Even though truss-frame building is economical, incredibly fast, energy efficient (trusses allow increased amounts of insulation to be built in), code approved, and backed by research and performance data gathered by the federal government, trade associations, and builders, it is in limbo. Yet the system has a lot to offer.

The most sensible way for interested home buyers and owner/builders to find information about truss framing is to contact the Wood Truss Council of America to obtain their list of truss-frame fabricators, then investigate designs and costs. The NAHB Research Foundation can also supply a limited list of builders who have used the system.

Since it is difficult to generate interest in the skeleton beneath the skin, this innovative building system may be passed over unless consumers prove that builders and developers are not correct in assuming that home buyers are willing to judge a book only by its cover.

For more information, request a copy of the well-illustrated forty-eight-page manual, called "Truss-Frame Construction," available for $5 from the NAHB Research Foundation Inc., Box 1627, Rockville, MD 20850. Although the Forest Products Laboratory has, technically, passed the truss-frame program on to the construction industry, its engineers have the best firsthand information on the subject (Forest Products Laboratory, Box 5130, Madison, WI 53705). Reprints of articles on the subject and additional referrals may be obtained through the Forest Service's Office of Information in Washington, 202-447-3957.

JUST ASK

Q I have received several reroofing estimates, but all in very confusing and even contradictory language. Some talk about square footage; others say squares of roof. One says 325-pound shingles; another, 205-pound. How do you compare these apples and oranges?

A Aside from listing the shingle manufacturer, fire-rating class, color, and style, roofing estimates must specify shingle weight and the amount needed to do the job. Shingle weight is expressed in pounds. Your roofers may have different opinions about how heavy a shingle to use. But as a rule, heavy shingles are thicker and last longer than light shingles, a fact that should be reflected in the warranties for the different weights.

A "square" in roofing language is actually 100 square feet. It's simply a convenient form of measurement and standard in the trade, so it's a bit odd that you got one estimate in square feet. Typically, labor and materials are included in a price per square, which is multiplied by the total number of squares needed to arrive at the total job cost.

Don't be confused by the different number of bundles (a standard package of shingles) per square. One square of heavy (and thick) 325-pound shingles, for example, will be packaged in four bundles. But a square of shingles in the 200-pound range comes in three bundles because the shingles are lighter and thinner.

2

THE LANGUAGE OF LUMBER

How to Tell the Board Feet from the Square Feet

Saturday morning you head off to the lumberyard with a shopping list of wood and nails and concrete in your hand and a plan for building two new porch steps in your mind. Full of optimism and enthusiasm, you are eager to get started. And the first step, ordering the materials, seems so simple.

But for amateur carpenters and inexperienced do-it-yourselfers alike that first step has two potential pitfalls. First, you may get the wrong materials. That can make the job unnecessarily difficult and the finished product needlessly inferior, even unsafe. Second, by using the wrong terminology, fumbling with crude drawings, or pantomiming hand signals to describe what you want, you can get the wrong materials and an acute inferiority complex.

Somehow do-it-yourselfers are supposed to know the difference between a common nail and a box nail and if sixpenny or tenpenny is the right size for the job, if the pine shelving should be clear or select, and if its price is based on square feet, linear feet, or board feet. Not knowing makes you vulnerable to unscrupulous salespeople who may recommend unnecessarily expensive

Lumber for today's houses ranges from seasoned logs in log homes to highly processed plywood beams such as these made by Trus Joist Corp.

materials. Not knowing makes you dependent on the goodwill of salespeople who may not have the time or patience to decipher your plans. Not knowing can also make you feel very uncomfortable.

Using appropriate language is an important do-it-yourself skill. Knowing every little detail isn't necessary, although being able to place an accurate order for materials is a very fundamental first step in any project. And if you hire professionals to do the work, a few pointed questions get their attention and signal that you have a good sense of what the job is and how work should progress.

Here is a look at some of the most common Saturday morning stumbling blocks, the points of confusion that may make you buy twice the wood you need or send the yard man on an extensive search for quarter-sawn boards that do not resemble the quarter-round ones you needed.

First you have to decipher the different types of lumberyard measurement. Lumber may be sold by the linear foot, square foot, or board foot. Linear-foot prices for lumber (and other materials commonly sold by length such as gutters and downspouts) work exactly as you would imagine. The unit price per linear foot, sometimes called a running foot, is multiplied by the number of feet you're buying, whether it's a stick of quarter round or Roman ogee molding.

Square-foot prices are commonly used on sheet materials such as plywood. Length times width determines overall size and price regardless of thickness. But 128 square feet of ¼-inch underlayment sheeting will cost much less per square foot than 128 square feet of ¾-inch birch veneer, furniture-quality plywood. Still, it's easy enough to measure the kitchen floor, for example, and bring home the right amount of material to cover it.

The most common form of measurement, used for most lumber, is also the most confusing. A board-foot measurement, unlike square-foot measurement, does take thickness into account. This makes the overall measurement of 1-inch-thick material completely different from the same-shape lumber in ½- or 2-inch thicknesses.

Technically, a board foot is a 12-inch length of 12-inch long, 1-inch thick material. A 1-foot length of 1-by-12-inch pine shelving would be 1 board foot, for example. But a 12-inch length of 2-by-6 timber would also measure 1 board foot. It's only half as wide but twice as thick. In neat multiples and halves, this system is easy to keep track of. Once you get into 2-by-10s, and mixed orders of 1-inch- and 2-inch-thick materials, it gets crazy.

To sort out the different sizes, use this formula:

$$\frac{\text{width (inches)} \times \text{thickness (inches)} \times \text{length (feet)}}{12}$$

For example, if you were buying a 24-inch length of 1-by-12 shelving, the formula would be: width (12) × thickness (1) × length (2; this dimension is listed in feet, not inches) divided by 12; 12 × 1 × 2 is 24 divided by 12, or 2 board feet. If you were buying a 36-inch length of 2-by-4 to support part of the shelf, the formula would be: width (4) × thickness (2) × length (3; in feet) divided by 12; 4 × 2 × 3 is 24 divided by 12, or 2 board feet. Two different lengths and thicknesses can be the same size measured by the board foot.

There is one giant hitch to this system. All those measurements are called "nominal." It's the lumber industry's way of saying that's what the lumber used to measure in its raw, rough-cut state before it was "dressed"—a strange way to define the process of trimming the board and making it smaller. That smaller, trimmed measurement is called the "actual" dimension. This means that a

2-by-4, nominally, is 2 by 4 inches, but 1½ by 3½ inches actually. Nominal measurements are used for pricing. (It figures, right?) So don't expect to get what you pay for, at least not actually.

The best analogy is probably to the English language in which there are overall rules, rules for the exceptions, and, of course, exceptions to the rules. With some sheet materials, for instance, the nominal dimension of 4-by-8 feet is also the actual dimension. Worse yet, on some long timbers such as 20-foot 2-by-10s, the 2-by-10 dimensions are nominal (1½-by-9½ actual), while the 20-foot dimension isn't actual or nominal. (It's common for long timbers to be ½ inch or so longer than the nominal dimension.)

Until you become familiar with the home center or lumberyard and with the people who run it, bring a ruler along with your shopping list of materials. Walk around the stacks of timbers; measure them, actually. Then ask the salesperson for the price per board foot (for almost all timbers), per linear foot for molding and other long, thin lengths, or per square foot for sheet materials.

Checking from one yard to another, you may find a substantial difference between prices and premiums placed on wide timbers or long lengths. Also, if you are ordering materials for a large project, ask about discounts. Almost all yards have three sets of prices: one for small-order retail customers; one for contractors buying materials for one or two jobs at a time; and one for builders buying materials for one or more complete houses at a time. You won't get that third-level price. But on an order for a large deck or a room addition, for instance, you should push for an improvement on the first-level retail price.

JUST ASK

Q How can I cut down on sound transmission between rooms? The partition walls are wood frame with ½-inch drywall on both sides.

A You can redecorate rooms to make them acoustically "soft." Think of sound as water and sound-deadening materials as sponges. Hard, slick surfaces that repel water also repel sound. Soft, porous surfaces such as wall-to-wall carpeting, drapes, and upholstered furniture soak up sound and make a room quieter.

It also helps to isolate sound. The most elaborate design is a double-stud wall with staggered 2-by-4 studs that eliminate the solid connections between drywall panels. Nailing 1-by-2 furring strips across the studs parallel to the floor is an easier, less expensive way to get nearly the same effect. Fill the spaces between furring strips with insulation before covering with drywall or paneling. Rigid foam panels wrapped in fabric and tacked directly to existing walls may reduce transmission by at least 35–40 decibels, making normal conversations inaudible in the next room.

3

BUILDING IN WINTER

Treated Wooden Foundations Make It Possible and Economical

As long ago as 1924, in a study of the construction industry, the federal government recorded a decrease in construction productivity during winter months. It's not surprising that many operations (e.g., excavating frozen ground and pouring concrete in below-freezing temperatures) are particularly difficult. Even such simple tasks as hammering a nail are tough. Cold weather also increases construction costs by at least 5 percent in most regions.

Since then, several preventive measures have been introduced that can reduce the problems of winter building and permit a head start on the spring surge of new construction. Concrete additives can shorten hardening time and prevent freezing. Wall sections can be shop built, then trucked to the site for quick assembly.

But the most far-reaching improvement in winter building is a wooden foundation system (yes, wood, not masonry). Until recently, it was known as the all-weather wood foundation.

The new name, permanent wood foundation (PWF), was developed by the wood industry in response to consumer and builder resistance to the idea of burying wood in the ground and expecting it to hold up a house. Builders are especially hesitant to adopt the system. Focus groups conducted by the American Plywood Association, including a session with Washington builders, found that while contractors understand the PWF system and believe that the specially treated wood panels will do the job of poured concrete or concrete block, they don't think home buyers will accept the idea.

One Iowa builder takes potential buyers into a slightly damp and chilly concrete block room, then into a dryer, warmer PWF room for comparison. But even though the PWF system is less expensive than conventional masonry, the builder charges more for it. Apparently, when the savings were passed along, buyers assumed the less expensive wood was inferior to the more expensive masonry, even when they had seen and felt the advantages of a PWF firsthand.

The wood framing and plywood sheathing used in the permanent wood foundation system is pressure treated with preservatives to resist rot.

The PWF may suffer from a lack of creative public relations work but not from a lack of technical support and field testing. Several trade associations actively support the system, which is now code approved in every state and in Canada, where approximately 10 percent of all single-family housing built in 1984 was built on wood foundations. (Since the PWF compares most favorably with masonry in cold climates and on remote sites where trucking in concrete is a problem, its use has developed most rapidly in the northern United States and Canada.)

Chemical wood preservatives injected throughout both the structural timbers and facing panels of the foundation system enable the wood to maintain structural integrity and resist decay. Buyers should be aware that the Environmental Protection Agency (EPA) is constantly reviewing the effects of chemical preservatives in residential applications. It's a good idea to check on the latest regulations and restrictions with the EPA and the builder before you choose to build a PWF home.

A typical PWF wall sits on a gravel footing. A wide, pressure-treated board called a mud sill rests on the gravel and supports a relatively conventional stud wall built of pressure-treated 2-by-6s, 24 inches on center. Treated plywood sheathing covers the frame. Before earth is backfilled against the wood foundation, plastic sheeting is draped over the wood, and drain tile is set in the gravel base near the mud sill to facilitate drainage.

The PWF system is usually, although not always, faster and less expensive to construct than masonry. An experienced crew working with prefabricated concrete forms might beat a crew of carpenters assembling a PWF frame on site, but when PWF panels are shop built and trucked to the site, excavation work, foundation walls, first-floor joists, and plywood decking can be completed by a crew in one long day. There are other advantages, too.

- Since no concrete is needed, a sudden drop in temperature, even a downpour, need not halt work.
- Wood-frame foundation walls are more resilient than rigid masonry and can withstand soil pressures, even moderate settling that could crack concrete or block walls.
- The conventional stud-wall configuration is easily insulated. Batts of fiberglass rated at approximately 3.5 R value per inch produce a foundation wall with at least an R-19 rating.
- The frame foundation has space for pipes and wires that would have to be exposed or set only in the first-floor frame when masonry foundation walls are used.

Specific cost savings compared with masonry for initial construction and continuing energy use are difficult to average in a meaningful way. For one thing, concrete costs and availability varies widely. Generally, the PWF is most cost-effective in cold climates and where concrete costs are high. For example, in Anchorage, where concrete is expensive, temperatures are low, and the building season is very short, about half of all new residences are built on wood foundations.

As more consumers become aware of the system and more builders realize that their clients will appreciate the advantages offered by PWF, the system should become more popular. The American Plywood Association estimates that the stock of roughly ninety thousand PWF homes will increase by ten thousand this year. The association sees PWF construction as one of the fastest-growing alternatives to conventional single-family and multifamily building.

There are several trade associations that provide information on the PWF system. The American Plywood Association (Box 11700, Tacoma, WA 98411) offers fifteen different publications on PWF. (Ask for the whole package—it's free—particularly the thirty-five-page brochure "Permanent Wood Foundation System.") The Southern Forest Products Association (Box 52468, New Orleans, LA 70152) offers a detailed booklet "Cost Saver Series No. 5: PWF Systems." The National Forest Products Association (1619 Massachusetts Ave. NW, Washington, DC 20036) offers a comprehensive and relatively technical manual on the system for $15 called "DFI Manual Report No. 7," just in case you want to see everything there is to see on the subject.

JUST ASK

Q A new garage roof installed over worn roll roofing has stopped leaks in the ceiling. But why do I still get dripping and dark stains along the outside overhangs when the job was done a month ago?

A On reroofing jobs it is common practice to install new drip edge (an L-shaped strip of aluminum flashing) along the edges of low-slope roofs. Most roofers nail the strips on first, cover the exposed edge with tar, then lay the new roofing. But some roofers apply the roofing, then the flashing, tarring over exposed seams and nail heads.

The first method seems to work better, particularly when the flashing and roofing are fully embedded in tar. Expansion and contraction of the metal, and direct exposure to weather, can cause cracks and then leaks in the surface-mounted flashing. That would produce the drips and stains you see from below.

To improve this type of installation, trowel a thin coat of roof tar over the flashing seam, embed a layer of 3- to 4-inch fiberglass roofing tape (it looks like a wide-weave burlap), and topcoat with roof cement to finish.

STEEL FRAMING

Out of the Skyscraper and into the House

Unlike wood, it doesn't warp, shrink, or split. Termites and carpenter ants can't chew through it. It's much lighter than masonry and it's easier and faster to assemble the pieces into a shelter. And it won't rot or crumble or burn. What probably sounds like the ultimate answer to prevent all kinds of home-maintenance and repair problems is steel framing—a residential version of the familiar structural skeletons of bridges and skyscrapers.

In this lighter-duty application of metal framing, connections between structural members are crimped or screwed together instead of riveted. The engineering system is similar to wood construction, organizing a system of sticks (whether wood or steel) into a cohesive frame. But the cutting, fitting, and joining is unfamiliar to do-it-yourselfers, homeowners, and many contractors who were brought up on hammer and nail. But because of its strength and durability (during a fire it can extend the time of possible escape before walls collapse) steel framing is the standard in commercial construction.

It is not financially competitive with conventional wood framing

New designs such as this Tri–Steel-built home use stucco, clapboards, and other materials over steel framing that doesn't rot, warp, or burn.

nationwide. It may never be in the Northwest, where abundant timber supplies are close at hand. But in some housing markets, particularly where construction timbers must be shipped in, which raises transportation costs and the final price of housing, steel and wood produce roughly equivalent square-foot costs. Steel framing is also used more in the South, where problems with mildew and rot have led many homeowners to perceive wood structures as temporary compared to masonry or steel.

But if steel offers so many advantages, why is it used in only 5 percent of residential building frames? For one thing, steel is a lot less accommodating than wood, which can often be coaxed and nudged into proper position. (In fact, a large sledgehammer used for shifting slightly out of plumb corner posts back into position is called a "persuader" by many carpenters.) Steel construction also requires tools and skills quite different (though not necessarily more complicated) than wood framing, which is a disadvantage for do-it-yourselfers.

The basic steel "timber" is three-sided; a 2-by-10-inch floor joist, for example, would have two narrow 2-inch edges (top and bottom) connected by only a single 10-inch side, creating a shallow U-shape. Connectors are available in all sorts of shapes to join the three-sided framing members. With solid wood, nails are driven through the thickness of one board into another. But the steel is in sheet form, from 12- to 25-gauge thickness (roughly .08–.02 inch). In a typical right-angle framing joint, one side of an L-shaped bracket is screwed to each steel member to make the connection.

Despite a familiar assembly sequence, metal shears, hacksaws, and self-tapping sheet metal screws are foreign objects to many amateur and professional carpenters. In fact, the National Association of Homebuilders reports that while the use of metal framing is growing in multifamily housing, single-family builders are reluctant to adopt new tools and methods of construction unless they offer a dramatic improvement over conventional and familiar wood framing.

At some point, many more builders may have to make the adjustment. Despite reassuring programs of reforestation and successful experiments in accelerated growth to produce mature trees at a faster rate than Mother Nature, our wood resources are declining. The NAHB reports that increasing amounts of wood are used in construction, and that wood and its by-products are used by a growing number of industries. Also, there is no longer a backlog of large trees that produce great amounts of good-quality structural timbers, at least not in commercial forestlands. It's as though rainfall is replenishing almost all the water drawn from a well while the water table supporting the well gradually declines.

Don't rush out and stock up on 2-by-4s. The NAHB says that short of extreme and unexpected market conditions that would make lumber costs prohibitive compared to the relatively stable costs of steel 2-by-4s, it could be twenty to thirty years before steel framing is used in even 25 percent of new residential construction. Surprisingly, there are few other alternatives.

Instead of wood floors, there is vinyl sheeting and ceramic tile and carpeting (even though there may be plywood underneath). Instead of wood siding, there is aluminum and vinyl. Instead of wood shakes on the roof, there is a wide selection of asphalt-based products. Even a lot of furniture traditionally made of wood is now plastic or inferior wood grades covered by laminates. But aside from steel, masonry continues to be the only significant alternative to wood framing.

There is some experimentation, predominantly in Japan, with

ceramic and plastic framing, similar to steel in configuration, using relatively thin sheet material shaped into reinforced panels. But there are drawbacks to this approach, including potentially lethal contributions to a fire and the staggering task of convincing consumers to buy a ceramic or plastic house.

Under the surface of new apartments or condominiums, however, it is increasingly likely that you'll find a steel frame. One firm, Cleaver Steel of Austin, Texas, has had success with shop-built (prefabricated) steel roof trusses and wall sections in substantial projects such as forty-building condominium complexes with five to nine units per building—even when staggered roof lines call for twelve different truss sizes ranging from 15- to 45-foot spans.

Aaron Cleaver reports that even in the hotbed of construction between Dallas and Ft. Worth, steel is very competitive with wood. On an $80,000 house, where framing might cost approximately $7,000–$10,000, using steel instead of wood might raise construction costs by $1,000. Mr. Cleaver notes that on houses with intricate floor plans and roof lines this figure will increase.

But Cleaver says his firm can equal or underbid commercial buildings built with wood frames, using 2-by-6-inch steel beams where 2-by-8s or 2-by-10s would be needed in wood. (Pound for pound, steel is 60 percent stronger than wood.) Also, because steel is available in different gauges, strength requirements can be tailored to the job. For example, on a wood-frame building, solid 2-by-4s required on exterior bearing walls are also used on non-load-bearing interior partition walls. But with steel construction a 3½- or 6-inch exterior wall stud can be heavy, 20-gauge material, while the same-shape studs in more economical and lighter-weight 25-gauge can be used on partition walls.

You won't find a wide selection of steel framing at the local lumberyard. But it is worth considering on a new building, even an addition, where the stability, strength, and fire safety of steel framing can make the structure last longer, require less maintenance and repair, and even reduce the rates for fire insurance.

For more information about steel trusses and framing members and referrals to other sources, contact Cleaver Steel, PO Box 2061, Austin, TX 78768.

JUST ASK

Q I am installing wallboard in a renovated attic above the garage and have run into trouble with the taping compound. No matter how carefully I apply it, it cracks and crumbles in some areas. Is it too hot or moist to tape now?

A That might be the problem. Most manufacturers suggest that temperature be maintained between 55° and 70° F and that the area be well ventilated. Fluctuations above and below these limits could cause the cracking. The crumbling is more likely a result of incomplete mixing.

When taping compound is mixed from scratch, it is common for tiny pockets of the powder to remain suspended in the mix even when the compound appears to be thoroughly combined to make an appropriately soupy consistency. After you've stirred and stirred, go again in the opposite direction and lift up compound from the bottom of the container, stirring up and down as well as around and around. Even premixed compound should be restirred before using.

SEPTEMBER

1 ENTER THE HOME INSPECTOR:
Getting a Pro to Check Out Your Prospective Home

Prospective home buyers tend to get caught up in the purchase price and the stress of relocating. That's why they consult the pros on the nitty-gritty questions. How much is the house worth? Ask an appraiser. How fair is the asking price? Ask a real estate agent. But

2 HIRING HOME PROFESSIONALS:
Issues Not Covered in the Contract

Homeowners must deal with many housing professionals, from arborists to well drillers—almost from A to Z. Even renters, who supposedly do not have the burdens of ownership, require the services of painters, floor sanders, a real estate attorney to check provisions

3 FINDING A CONTRACTOR YOU CAN COUNT ON:
Picking the Right Apple from the Barrel

It is increasingly difficult to find and hire a good carpenter or general contractor. Many home consumers who have a long-term relation-

4 ASKING QUESTIONS OF THE EXPERTS:
Since You're Paying the Bill, You're Entitled

The so-called consumer movement has encouraged us to be selective, to ask questions, acquire information, look critically at advertis-

Home Professionals

what about the physical condition of a house? That's a loaded question —loaded with unknowns that can dramatically alter the true long-term cost of any home, old or new. Enter yet another real estate professional: the home inspector. An inspector must have technical knowledge and practical experience to evaluate a house—also absolutely no stake in the results of the evaluation.

of a lease, and others. While most consumers are now familiar with safeguards such as contacting the local Better Business Bureau and consumer protection agency, there are seven areas where even a thorough selection process can be undermined. Here are the seven deadly sins and how to avoid the sometimes subtle traps they can set for homeowners and apartment dwellers alike.

ship with a family doctor, a dentist, or an accountant simply do not know how to find someone to fix squeaking floors or build a new porch railing, much less a new addition. Hiring a reliable and qualified contractor is a time-consuming process. You have to develop leads, track down referrals, verify recommendations, and conduct face-to-face interviews. Then, too, the number of carpenters and general contractors who know whole-house construction from foundation to roof has declined.

ing, and comparison shop—all before making a final decision to buy a particular product. But for all the emphasis on self-help and doing it yourself, many consumers still want an expert to tell them exactly what to do. What could be easier than getting a little exercise? Yet countless spas and gyms and sports clubs with regimented programs flourish. Whether it's gardening, weight watching, or investing money, too often an "informed consumer" takes the word of an expert on blind faith. This is often the case with homeowners trying to line up housing services.

1

ENTER THE HOME INSPECTOR

Getting a Pro to Check Out Your Prospective Home

Prospective home buyers tend to get caught up in the purchase price and the stress of relocating. That's why they consult the pros on the nitty-gritty questions. How much is the house worth? Ask an appraiser. How fair is the asking price? Ask a real estate agent.

But what about the physical condition of a house? That's a loaded question—loaded with unknowns that can dramatically alter the true long-term cost of any home, old or new.

Knowing a home's value in dollars and cents is important; the numbers can be deceptively clean and theoretical. On the other hand, the condition of foundations, framing, interiors, and mechanical systems has a very real impact on repair costs, utility bills, maintenance time, your sense of satisfaction, even your safety. Knowing the physical state of the structure is crucial. The goal is to find out about it before you buy, not after you move in.

Enter yet another real estate professional: the home inspector.

Many in the field use that title, although others can do the job just as well. General building contractors, architects, and engineers who regularly work on the type of property you're considering should be well qualified.

An inspector must have technical knowledge and practical experience to evaluate a house—also absolutely no stake in the results of the evaluation. This criterion eliminates the real estate agent who makes money if you decide to buy, even though some of his suggestions about repairs and upkeep may be helpful. It also eliminates real estate attorneys and mortgage lenders, who probably do not have the know-how in any case.

A home inspector works for you, the potential buyer. You, not an agent or attorney or banker, should interview, hire, and pay the inspector. The price should be based on a flat fee, not a percentage of the sale price or on how many problem areas are discovered. Standards for home inspections and inspectors have been established by the American Society of Home Inspectors (ASHI),

The home inspector you hire, whether a contractor, architect, or engineer, should have experience with the building system in question.

founded in 1976. The Society's full members, many of whom are engineers, have performed at least four hundred inspections and have the education or experience equivalent of six hundred more.

This kind of practice certainly helps, although time spent on construction, repair, or maintenance work is the real key. A good inspector will quickly recognize telltale signs of trouble—for example, dark-ringed water spots on the ceiling that indicate a roof leak, not condensation.

Reports that a faucet doesn't turn or a door doesn't close completely are not terribly helpful. You can discover tidbits like that by yourself. The question is why. Is the plumbing generally inferior, of substandard capacity, clogged with mineral deposits, patched and repatched from leaks? Or is the problem simply a frozen faucet handle that can be replaced for only a few dollars?

For all its standards, ASHI literally excludes from inspection nearly as much as it includes. For example, the plumbing system is covered but not well-water quality or septic systems. However, ASHI members I've talked to conduct more thorough inspections than these forms may lead you to believe.

When you are shopping for an inspector, ask for a sample inspection report. Looking through it, you can judge if the type of detailed information it contains would be of help to you. Avoid inspections that consist of a simple checklist, no matter how long it is; checklist forms tend to be extremely generic, with a poor-to-excellent type of status report on each item that offers little, if any, practical help.

Depending on the size and complexity of the house, an inspection may cost from $100 to $300; it should be a typewritten evaluation filled with usable details.

Suppose the inspection uncovers the fact that key girders and beams supporting an exterior deck show signs of dry rot and that the supporting concrete piers are cracked and unstable. This information can serve as the basis for a very specific home repair estimate from a contractor. And that dollar figure, supported by a contractor's finding and the written inspection report, can provide ammunition during sale price negotiations.

In fact, that is the best way to reduce an asking price: not by complaining or picking a lower number arbitrarily but by proving that a portion of the purchase price will have to be used to make right what is wrong.

This written report becomes your property. It should be considered confidential and shared with the seller or seller's agents only as you see fit. And remember, it is just as important to know what's right about your house as what's wrong.

For information on inspection standards and a referral to local ASHI-affiliated inspectors, write the American Society of Home Inspectors, Suite 520, 1629 K St. NW, Washington, DC 20006.

JUST ASK

Q Just in time for winter my twenty-year-old roof has sprung two leaks. One roofer says he can solve the problem by patching with roof cement and a few new shingles. Another says I need a new roof. Who is right?

A Both roofers may be right. Although your first roof is no doubt reaching the end of its useful life span, patches made by setting new shingles in a bed of roof tar to replace damaged and leaking sections is a reasonable short-term solution. This inexpensive repair may last several years—until everyone agrees that the roof needs to be replaced as in stage 4 of this typical deteriorization sequence.

Stage 1: Surface granules (the tiny chips embedded in shingles) accumulate in gutters and downspout outlets.

Stage 2: Bare patches of black tar appear as more granules are lost, a very recognizable symptom on white- or gray-surfaced shingles.

Stage 3: Shingle tabs (the part of a shingle exposed to the weather) become brittle and curl into a convex shape.

Stage 4: Brittle curled tabs break off and bare tar patches wear so that nail heads and seams normally covered are exposed.

At stages 1 and 2, patching may be reasonable. At stage 3, and certainly at stage 4, a new roof is a more cost effective alternative.

2

HIRING HOME PROFESSIONALS:

Issues Not Covered in the Contract

Homeowners must deal with many housing professionals, from arborists to well drillers—almost from A to Z. Even renters, who supposedly do not have the burdens of ownership, require the services of painters, floor sanders, a real estate attorney to check provisions of a lease, and others. While most consumers are now familiar with safeguards such as contacting the local Better Business Bureau and consumer protection agency, there are seven areas where even a thorough selection process can be undermined.

Here are the seven deadly sins and how to avoid the sometimes subtle traps they can set for homeowners and apartment dwellers alike.

1. *Failure to Trust Your Instincts.* In almost all cases, home professionals know more—probably a lot more—about the subject than home consumers who may hire them. In the struggle to understand unfamiliar ideas, much less the terminology of materials and construction techniques, too many consumers

forget about the most important part of the job—the person doing the work.

Professional qualifications aside, is the roofer reasonably friendly? Do you feel comfortable about this person coming to your home? These questions may turn out to be just as important as questions about the professional's expertise.

You don't have to become best friends, but you must be able to communicate with home professionals. And it's difficult to have a productive conversation with someone who is irritating or obnoxious or who, for some reason, just rubs you the wrong

Although building and real estate matters are complex, professionals should be able to explain their plan in plain, nontechnical language.

way. But you don't have to be a good judge of shingles to judge
the personality (or at least the compatibility) of a shingler. If
you walk away from the first meeting with an uncomfortable
feeling that you can't pin down, trust your instincts and talk
to another roofer.

2. *Stifling Competition.* Even though it can be difficult to arrange for several carpenters to arrive during the same week
to bid on the same job, try to arrange it. Competition is healthy.
Don't undercut capitalism at work by signing with the first
person who shows up. Arriving at a prescribed hour to give an
estimate is not necessarily a precursor of good miter joints.

Try to get three estimates for major projects. And it doesn't
hurt to let each bidder know there are two other candidates. In
fact, if there are discrepancies in the bids (one carpenter may
suggest using 2-by-10 joists while another specifies 2-by-8s, for
instance), you can ask each bidder to comment on the other's
proposal. This cross-checking (without disclosing the entire estimate to the competition) can be done in a good-natured way
and usually elicits an informative response.

3. *Bending under Pressure.* No one wants to miss out on a good
thing, a special deal, a one-time-only price. But although common sense indicates that there is no good reason for a basement
waterproofing job to cost $1,200 on Monday and considerably
more by Wednesday, too many consumers are still suckered by
deals that, in retrospect, were too good to be true.

If the contractor can only start work immediately or you
have to act now to get free materials left over from another
job or if the plumbing fixtures you're considering are just
about due for a major price increase, hesitate. For the one
case where you actually will lose out on a legitimate low bid
or a surprisingly low sale price, there are a hundred instances
where hesitating under pressure will save you from trouble.
Almost always there is a very good reason for a very low
price: the "special" furnace model is being discontinued by
the manufacturer; the low-cost 2-by-4s are heavy with moisture and ready to twist and warp.

Home professionals should tell you about their products and
services. And it's natural for them to make the best possible
impression by stressing advantages, not drawbacks. But when
strong selling becomes strong pressure to close the deal, don't
bend.

4. *Confusing Supply and Demand.* Consumers are all too familiar with the law of supply and demand: They have an unending

demand for an extensive supply of goods and services. But when you want to hire a surveyor or an exterminator, remember that you and your property and your termites are the supply for the professional's demand for work.

Don't underestimate the power this gives you. If mortgage rates drop two points as the spring building season approaches, the law of supply and demand may work against you, making it impossible to find a builder who returns phone calls. But often, and particularly out of the busy building season, the balance tips as the home professional's demand for work outweighs the supply of clients. That's when you'll get more attention and lower estimates.

5. *Gambling.* Older, more established contractors, real estate agents, and other professionals tend to be harder to get and considerably more expensive than people just getting started in business. But the fact that a firm has lasted for several decades is usually a positive sign, particularly in home repair and construction fields where word-of-mouth recommendations can make or break a reputation quickly.

Eagerness, energy, and a wall covered with degrees and credentials all indicate that the job should work out satisfactorily. An established track record shows that many jobs similar to yours already have worked out. The U.S. Army advertising slogan "We don't ask for experience; we give it" may be fine for raw recruits but not for raw consumers. Don't be a guinea pig for inexperienced home professionals. Paying less to people with less experience is a gamble with bad odds.

6. *Nodding without Knowing.* In polite conversation it may be safe to nod in agreement even when you didn't quite understand the last half of the sentence. Usually, the next sentence helps you fill in the blanks and avoids embarrassing misunderstandings. But when a builder runs on about CDX sheathing and FC drywall and GFCI breakers, it's a mistake to agree amiably with the insiders' language. Sometimes you may agree unwittingly to needlessly expensive alterations and additions.

You're the client. You're paying the bill. That entitles you to ask questions. If the answers are too technical, ask for a better explanation. If you can't get an answer that makes sense, ask someone else.

7. *Failure to Get It in Writing.* This sin is so obvious, so fundamental, that everyone should know about it and avoid it. But they don't. Too often a homeowner who wouldn't consider giving money to a builder for an addition without a detailed con-

tract will hire someone to fix the roof or add an outlet based on a handshake. It's a friendly gesture that can lead to completely avoidable misunderstandings.

Writing down a verbal agreement forces both parties to clarify their expectations. It uncovers misunderstandings on paper before they are literally set in cement. While a written contract for a new house or major addition is lengthy and complex, a simple, short letter of agreement will do for small jobs.

In its most basic form, to cover the most inconsequential jobs, the letter simply identifies both parties, the job in question, the price, and method of payment. A more complete letter, including product guarantees, contractor's liability insurance, a detailed listing of materials, and other points, may be more appropriate for larger jobs. No contractor should object to writing down verbal promises. They should be ready to put it all in writing and then shake on the deal.

JUST ASK

Q How can I compare the cost and efficiency of furnaces, wood stoves, and other appliances that use different fuels? It seems every salesman uses comparisons that favor the unit and fuel he's selling. I'm getting lost comparing apples and oranges.

A Here's one guideline for comparing heat sources: One cord of hardwood equals one ton of coal equals 200 gallons of fuel oil equals 4,000 kwh of electricity. There are too many variables (such as the cost per kwh) to make this more than a rough guideline. And it's even more difficult to calculate the heating benefits of wood. A cord (4-by-4-by-8 feet of stacked logs) of seasoned hardwood such as oak will produce about 23 million BTUs per cord, while the same amount of a soft wood such as aspen or basswood produces only about half as much.

To split hairs among production and efficiency rates of appliances using different fuels, the best bet is to use conversion factors—and a calculator. Conversion factors can be used to show heat equivalents in BTUs (British thermal units, the standard of heat measurement). For natural gas, multiply by 1,031 to find the BTUs per cubic foot. For electricity, multiply by 3,412 to find the BTUs per kwh. For number 2 fuel oil, figure 140,000 BTUs per gallon, or if you need an exact answer, 138,690.48.

Further insights into this question may be gained through energy equivalents—a series of strange but true comparisons compiled and published by the Energy Information Administration, a division of the Department of Energy. For example:

- One BTU equals the energy in one blue-tip kitchen match, or four-fifths of a peanut butter and jelly sandwich.
- One million BTUs equals 125 pounds of dried hardwood, 11 gallons of propane, or 240 bottles of table wine.
- One quadrillion BTUs equals 170 million barrels of crude oil, thirty-two days of U.S. petroleum imports, or thirty hours of world energy consumption.

3

FINDING A CONTRACTOR YOU CAN COUNT ON

Picking the Right Apple from the Barrel

It is increasingly difficult to find and hire a good carpenter or general contractor. Many home consumers who have a long-term relationship with a family doctor, a dentist, or an accountant simply do not know how to find someone to fix squeaking floors or build a new porch railing, much less a new addition.

Hiring a reliable and qualified contractor is a time-consuming process. You have to develop leads, track down referrals, verify recommendations, and conduct face-to-face interviews. Then, too, the number of carpenters and general contractors who know whole-house construction from foundation to roof has declined.

Specialization in the building trades, limited apprenticeship time, and two recent depressions in the building industry also have thinned the ranks. That's good in a way, because only the fittest, most diligent and established contractors can survive really hard times. But the builders who kept working through the housing bust in the early 1970s and the nearly 20 percent mortgage interest rates of only a few years ago are generally well-known—benefiting from widespread word-of-mouth recommendations—and booked solid.

An experienced general building contractor has the specialized equipment for the job, such as this collection of log-building tools.

There is an answer to this problem, but it is not self-contracting —which is all the rage now in how-to advice. The general idea behind acting as your own general contractor is to hire a team of subcontractors for specialized sections of the work, buy your own materials, and do the supervision in your spare time. This way, theoretically, you get things done the way you want and save 30 or 40 percent of job costs to boot. If this sounds realistic, even if you don't have construction experience, you might also be interested in buying this big bridge I own in Brooklyn.

General contracting requires common sense and some of the organizational skills we all have. But wouldn't you expect more than that from a professional who was working on your home? That word "general" means the contractor must know about framing and trimming and building codes and materials and a good deal more.

A general contractor sometimes may handle all the woodwork, hiring specialty subcontractors for plumbing and wiring, for example. Still, he must know about all the trades in order to put the pieces of the puzzle together. That takes more than common sense. It takes experience and judgment acquired from extensive time on the job.

There is another option. You could become a do-it-yourselfer, invest in power tools, take a crash course in construction, read every building book, then try your hand. That's fine if you have enough time and patience and potential skill to learn on the job and if you are willing to use your home as a guinea pig. On many jobs it is certainly worth a try.

But most home construction, repair, and improvement work is done by professionals. More than 75 percent of all money spent in these fields, with the single exception of interior painting, is spent on jobs done by contractors, not by do-it-yourselfers.

The trick is to find a professional you can count on. Ideally, you would get a firsthand recommendation from a neighbor, someone who has just had similar work done, who will show you the results and tell you about the costs, schedules, and more. But in most cases you have to search out several contractors, whittle down the list to two or three candidates, then ask for and evaluate estimates.

Develop a list using referrals and recommendations. Referrals are neutral, just names you get from ads, professional societies, trade associations, and the like. Use the *Encyclopedia of Associations* in a local library, area chapters of trade unions, even the Yellow Pages, to get started.

Recommendations are more valuable because they carry an evaluation. If you can't get them from a friend, try disinterested home professionals with nothing to gain by providing a name. Ask your home insurance agent, real estate agent, mortgage banker, a building inspector, and others. Scrutinize even more carefully the names provided by potentially interested parties—for example, a lumber dealer who may make a profit on materials if his recommendation gets the job.

A good choice results from good information. Remember that you are the one with the money. That gives you the right to ask questions and get reasonable answers before signing a contract. Any established contractor should be able, even eager, to document work experience with blueprints, photographs, and names of satisfied customers. Verify this documentation and check for complaints at the local Better Business Bureau and Consumer Protection Agency.

Once you've done the homework and found someone who does a good job at a good price, you may be reluctant to pass along their name too many times. (They may be too busy the next time you need them, right?) Consider this possibility: Put your carpenter or contractor on retainer. Once you've found a good one, why not agree to a service contract of sorts with regular payments. Add up all the money spent on repairs and maintenance annually, divide by 12, and make equal retainer payments every month.

Yes, it is a novel idea. But it should appeal to contractors who suffer the financial highs and lows of a seasonally sensitive profession. In return, you would be able to deal with one reliable contractor who comes to know the peculiarities of your home and who is accessible. This system has been applied successfully to legal and financial services, to lawn care, pest control, and the maintenance of major appliances of every description. Why not to the whole house?

For more information: Membership in a builder's organization does not guarantee quality construction. But it is a healthy sign. If you can't locate three or four local builders to bid on your construction project, the National Association of Home Builders can help. The NAHB provides referral services to some 130,000 members through 700 local chapters. In addition to conducting all kinds of construction research, the NAHB provides arbitration services and offers an interesting, whole-house warranty program through some of its members. Write the Director of Consumer Affairs, National Association of Home Builders, 15th and M streets NW, Washington, DC 20005.

JUST ASK

Q It appears that one of my new sliding-glass doors has come off the track. I know how to put a sliding screen back on its track, but the door doesn't seem to work the same way. Are there any tips that would help, or must I call the contractor back?

A A few small points may help. But they may not help if one of the wheels in the bottom of the door is broken. If the door is off the track now, carefully tip it onto one of the long edges and inspect the wheels concealed in the bottom rail. In most models there is a small carriage assembly attached to the aluminum or wood frame, often with an adjusting screw (usually with the head accessible from the door edge) for raising and lowering the wheel.

If the wheel is broken, write the manufacturer for a replacement or take the broken one into a home center or hardware store to be sure you get an exact match. If the wheel has worn or the carriage has sagged a bit, adjust the screw to lower the wheel, say, ⅛ inch. (Lowering the wheel raises the door, which may be catching on the sill.) This can be done when the door is on the track, too. But the door must first be "unloaded," which means using a crowbar, for example, to remove the weight of the door from the wheel.

Also check the ribbed channel on the doorsill along which the door glides. It would be unusual, but certainly possible, for the rib to be dented or bent in a way that makes the door bind or chatter during operation. To install a door in working order, the first step is to call a large friend, particularly if the door has double glazing. The trick is to set the groove cut into the upper edges of the door into the guide strip of metal in the top frame. Then, with the door nearly vertical, lift it and swing the bottom in the few inches necessary to set the wheels on their track. The upper groove is deep enough to accommodate this extra lift and still capture the guide strip after the door is lowered. This extra vertical play is why most patio doors are an easy target for burglars.

4

ASKING QUESTIONS OF THE EXPERTS

Since You're Paying the Bill, You're Entitled

The so-called consumer movement has encouraged us to be selective, to ask questions, acquire information, look critically at advertising, and comparison shop—all before making a final decision to buy a particular product.

But for all the emphasis on self-help and doing it yourself, many consumers still want an expert to tell them exactly what to do. What could be easier than getting a little exercise? Yet countless spas and gyms and sports clubs with regimented programs flourish. Whether it's gardening or weight watching or investing money, too often an "informed consumer" takes the word of an expert on blind faith. And too often this is the case with homeowners trying to line up housing services.

If you can find an expert whose advice produces good results once or twice—whether it's a magazine recommending an air conditioner or a real estate agent suggesting a particular parcel of land—it is tempting to rely on them without question. (In fact, trying to get your money's worth without them can seem like a full-time job.) And some experts don't like too many questions from consumers; they may act huffy or offended and can intimidate consumers into easy acquiescence by projecting an authoritarian, know-it-all image.

I call it the white-coat, blind-faith syndrome, demonstrated in an astonishing experiment conducted in 1965 by behavioral scientist Stanley Milgram. Unsuspecting subjects were told they would be part of a scientific learning experiment, scoring other people's answers to questions by working controls of scoring consoles that appeared to deliver electrical shocks for incorrect answers.

But the people "answering" the questions, out of view but in audio contact in an adjoining room, were in on the experiment; and the control panels were bogus, just lights and switches that didn't shock anyone. Every time an incorrect answer was reported, the participants who were scoring were supposed to flip a lever, working their way across the panel through switches that increased the voltage delivered after each wrong answer, all the way to a final switch labeled "Danger—Severe Shock."

When Milgram's cohorts deliberately answered questions incorrectly and then feigned pained shouts and even screams after the switches were thrown, many scorers hesitated. When they did, a "scientist" in a white lab coat entered the control room and told them to proceed with the experiment.

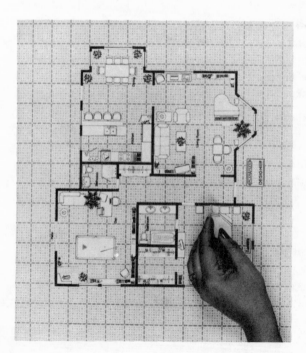

Cutout design kits such as the Plan-A-Flex Home Designer can help to show on paper at a small scale how a floor plan may work at full scale.

Amazingly, all the scorer subjects flipped switches labeled as high as 300 volts—the point at which Milgram's experimenters started yelling and banging on the connecting wall. Nevertheless, many scorers continued through the entire panel, often agonizing about the results of throwing the switches but with an authoritative direction to continue, throwing them, anyway.

In a disturbing documentary film of the experiment called *Obedience*, the scorers' hesitance and apprehension, their protestations and questioning, are subdued again and again by the authoritative figure, the official in the white coat who tells them what to do.

Everyone tends to think, "I would have gotten up and walked out," though only a few subjects did. But even a mild case of the white-coat, blind-faith syndrome can hurt. If a carpenter specifies $750 for fixing the porch, many consumers will pick the estimate apart, solicit competitive bids, and check costs at the lumberyard. But when a real estate attorney specifies $750 for a closing fee, most expectant homeowners do little more than grumble.

There is simply no substitute for asking questions and insisting on reasonable, understandable answers. Professional lingo is part of the white-coat mystique and should be dismissed as quickly as the puffery often heard in radio and television commercials; advice is certainly no more expert because it is offered in long-winded, technical gobbledygook. It's worth noting that *Popular Mechanics* magazine owed much of its initial success to the editorial philosophy included as a subtitle on covers of early issues: "Written So You Can Understand It."

When dealing with a housing professional, for example, a home insurance agent, prepare for face-to-face interviews by readying a list of specific questions. Ask for alternatives to the recommended coverage. Comparison shop at another agency. Compare the answers you get, and the prices. Better yet, challenge one agent to justify a higher price for what looks suspiciously like the same coverage offered by the competition.

Look for a clearly explained plan of action, not a reassuring smile and a leave-it-to-me pat on the back. Seek assurances from the professional about results. If you deal with a firm, find out who will perform the service—the branch manager you're talking to or a clerk who has just finished a training program.

Many consumers examine endless details of construction and performance before buying tangible housing products. It's worth the occasional ruffled feather to be just as vigilant with housing services.

For more information: One of the few consumer agencies in the country that recognizes that the best product is useless if an installer or serviceman botches the job is the Center for the Study of Services. The agency's local publication is called *Washington Consumer's Checkbook*. (They produce a similar quarterly in the San Francisco Bay area.) The organization is an excellent source for ratings of all kinds of consumer services, including long-distance phone companies. Write them at 806 15th St. NW, Suite 925, Washington, DC 20005.

JUST ASK

Q I wrote away for information on a time-sharing property. The literature I received uses the phrase "undivided interest" instead. What's the difference?

A In most cases time-sharing entitles you to share the property with others for a specific time. You might buy the second week in August in a vacation condominium, for example. It's like renting an apartment; you're entitled to stay there for the length of the lease, but that's all. If the apartment building doubles in value while you're there, the landlord gets the increased equity and all your rent. You get your security deposit back, maybe.

Buying an undivided interest in the property (generally more expensive than a time-sharing plan) is like buying a co-op or condominium. You actually own a piece of the project. Technically, an undivided interest gives each owner the right to use the entire property. But rules covering who gets what facilities for how long and when can differ greatly.

So before buying, check any sales prospectus and contract very carefully with a real estate attorney. Also, consider the proposition as a real estate investment, evaluating location, consumer demand, competition, the potential for appreciation, and more. Finally, consider how the carrying expenses (overnight charges and other use fees, maintenance charges, dues, etc., which can mount up) compare to the cost of similar services and accommodations on a more conventional, pay-as-you-go holiday.

OCTOBER

1 HOME MAINTENANCE FOR FALL:
Not Necessarily a Necessary Evil

Home maintenance is boring. It belongs in that special category of things to do that includes having semiannual dental checkups, filing quarterly tax estimates, and changing the oil in your car. But there is something worse: home replacements. Replacing a refrigerator

2 HOUSECLEANING SPECIALTIES:
Solutions for Stains, Scratches, Dents, and Dirt

Cleaning a house, and the furnishings and fixtures inside it, is a complicated business. The permutations of paint, wood, plastic laminate, and other materials stained with everything from ink to peanut butter and jelly seem to require hundreds of different cleaners. For

3 PLUMBING REPAIRS:
Solutions to Common Problems

Most parts of a residential plumbing system are out of sight and inaccessible, buried in the walls and floors. Before the framing is covered over, plumbers conduct a water test, literally filling up every pipe in the system, including vents, to test for leaks. Occasionally,

4 ELECTRICAL REPAIRS:
Solutions to Common Problems

Making repairs and improvements in electrical systems calls for caution and common sense. In fact, most consumers rate electrical projects right at the bottom of the list of do-it-yourself work, partly because wiring is complicated, partly because, unlike jobs such as

Maintenance and Repair

motor, a hot-water heater, or a rotting floorboard nets nothing more than a working version of what was there already. Replacements don't save money, add space, increase convenience, or build up home equity. Avoiding no-win replacement jobs can be the best motivation for doing preventive home-maintenance work, the latter clearly being the lesser of two evils.

every stain and type of dirt there are specialized cleaning products, including a constantly updated supply of new-and-improved ingredients with names normally reserved for experimental aircraft. The choices are staggering. But there is an alternative. Home remedies, using common household items (sometimes in slightly bizarre combinations), often equal or surpass the cleaning power of special preparations, and usually at considerably less expense.

part of the hidden system can break, for example, when cold weather freezes water in a supply pipe located in an exterior wall. But most plumbing problems are out in the open, in the fixtures.

painting and papering, electrical work is unforgiving and potentially dangerous. But good lighting is also a crucial ingredient of any successful addition or major alteration.

1

HOME MAINTENANCE
FOR FALL

Not Necessarily a Necessary Evil

Home maintenance is boring. It belongs in that special category of things to do that includes having semiannual dental checkups, filing quarterly tax estimates, and changing the oil in your car.

But there is something worse. It's not home repairs, which involve detective work, ingenuity, and the rewards of not having to fight with a bureau drawer that used to stick or a refrigerator that used to melt gallons of raspberry sherbet into the ice maker. And it's certainly not home improvements, which have many obvious rewards.

Replacements are the worst jobs. Replacing a refrigerator motor, a hot-water heater, or a rotting floorboard nets nothing more than a working version of what was there already. Replacements don't save money, add space, increase convenience, or build up home equity. Avoiding no-win replacement jobs can be the best motivation for doing preventive home-maintenance work, the latter clearly being the lesser of two evils.

In other words, even though airplane maintenance doesn't increase storage space or leg room, the drudgery of tightening and

Common fall maintenance jobs include clearing leaves from gutters and angled "offset" fittings between the roof edge and downspouts.

retightening the bolts on a jet engine sure beats dropping one somewhere over Kansas City.

Preventive maintenance should be ongoing (the way the airlines do it). But a seasonal schedule—three or four times a year—is as much as most people can manage, because maintenance has a low priority. It's like a long-term financial investment (in this case, buying future leisure time and extending product and material life spans)—the right thing to do only after more immediate concerns are cared for.

Since preventive-maintenance time is scarce, use it tending to items that would be missed if they didn't work correctly and would cost the most to repair or replace if they broke. Following that logic, the flaming orange-yellow leaves of fall are harbingers of flames in furnaces and wood stoves that provide winter comfort, even survival; uncontrolled by properly functioning appliances, flue pipes, and chimneys, those flames could lead to the biggest replacement job of all—rebuilding a fire-gutted house. That gives combustion heat sources the highest priority.

Here are a few guidelines on heating systems and other areas that may take priority in your home. (Be sure to break electrical connections before working on any appliance and remember that manufacturer's instructions supersede any general guidelines.)

- Hot-Air Heating. Replace furnace filters; vacuum dust from blower intake, squirrel cage, fan blades, and vent grills on motor housings. Lubricate motors (normally done through flapped oil cups with six drops of nondetergent electric-motor oil) and adjust blower-belt tension to about ¾-inch deflection under moderate pressure; replace cracked or frayed belts and store spare ones nearby. Also, clear dust from the cold-air return (usually an oversize register in a central location) and the system air cleaner if it does not have an automatic washing feature.
- Hot-Water Heating. Lubricate circulators (the torpedo-shaped motors above the furnace) with three or four drops of nondetergent electric-motor oil. On systems fed with relatively hard water (with a high mineral content) flush the entire system. In all cases, check for trapped air at radiators and convectors by "bleeding" air until water escapes from valves on or near these units. Clear air inlets at the base of room convectors and unsnap the "can" covers to vacuum between heat-dispersing fin plates.
- Steam Heating. Clean blocked valves by soaking them in vinegar overnight and clearing mineral deposits with a stiff brush. Eliminate pipe banging near radiators by adding a small block under radiator legs farthest away from the inlet pipe.
- Flue Pipes and Chimneys. Check soot dumps annually. (They are usually behind a small metal door near the chimney base.) Accumulations may signal inefficient combustion and oil-laden soot deposits in the furnace vent stack that can flash into puffbacks or ignite into dangerous fires. Flue pipes on furnaces and wood or coal stoves can be disassembled and brushed clean. Cover openings into masonry flues (the entire opening of a fireplace) before cleaning the chimney. Raising and lowering a sand-filled, heavy canvas bag through the flue provides a cursory cleaning. Generally, it makes more sense to hire a chimney sweep who is comfortable working up on the roof ridge and who uses special steel brushes to dislodge creosote buildup on flue liner walls that may not break loose with a homemade, sack-of-sand cleaning.

- Pipe Freezing. In chilly crawl spaces snap-on foam insulation tubes will protect cold-water pipes and reduce heat loss from hot-water pipes. Where freezing is a threat, spiral wrap pipes with thermostatic heat tapes. These plug into electrical outlets like extension cords; when the thermostat senses low temperature, the tapes draw current to make resistance heating (just enough to keep stationary cold water from solidifying). Open and drain exterior faucets, closing their supply valves inside the house. Also, clear water from hoses and sprinklers before storing in unheated areas.
- Gutters and Leaders. Clear leaves from gutters, then flush with a garden hose to confirm that downspouts and drains are free flowing. Blockages are most common at offset fittings where downspouts against the house wall connect to gutters along the roof overhang. For northside roofs where snow accumulates, consider heat tapes (very similar to the cables used to prevent pipe freezing) set in a zigzag pattern along the lower courses of the shingles. Resistance heat prevents ice dams that clog gutters, break downspouts, and lift shingles.

If you are at all unfamiliar with heat-system maintenance, contact your utility company or a heating contractor. Many offer seasonal start-up servicing on a contract basis—annually for oil systems, every two or three years for natural-gas systems.

For more information: Facts of the high-priority areas where controlling combustion is so important are available from the National Fire Protection Association, Batterymarch Park, Quincy, MA 02269. Noting the increase in owner-installed wood and coal stoves (in some states, New York, for example, new laws will require building permits and inspections for these installations), the NFPA has a list of publications, including "Save Home Energy the Firesafe Way" and "Home Heating Fact Sheet."

JUST ASK

Q Where can I tap into power lines that will run a door chime?

A Power comes from the standard house wiring system. But it must be "stepped down" with a transformer. In a typical installation a 10- or 24-volt transformer is connected to the house wiring inside a junction box. (Obviously, all power must be off before you touch the system, and for safety's sake, you should do so only if you are completely confident and familiar with the process.)

Low-voltage bell wire is used to make the connections between the button, chime unit, and transformer, not the thicker wiring used in the 120-volt house system. The only other pitfall can be avoided by making sure that the output voltage of the transformer matches the voltage rating of the chime. Note that some transformers can provide different voltages through different terminals on the same unit.

2

HOUSECLEANING SPECIALTIES

Solutions for Stains, Scratches, Dents, and Dirt

Cleaning a house, and the furnishings and fixtures inside it, is a complicated business. The permutations of paint, wood, plastic laminate, and other materials stained with everything from ink to peanut butter and jelly seem to require hundreds of different cleaners. For every stain and type of dirt there are specialized cleaning products, including a constantly updated supply of new-and-improved ingredients with names normally reserved for experimental aircraft. The choices are staggering. But there is an alternative.

Home remedies, using common household items (sometimes in slightly bizarre combinations), often equal or surpass the cleaning power of special preparations, and usually at considerably less expense. For example, if you have chlorine bleach, you probably do not have to buy a specialized mildew remover, toilet bowl cleaner, or sanitizing bathroom cleaner. If you have vinegar, you probably don't need to buy a sealer for plaster walls or a copper cleaner. If you have ammonia, you probably don't need several types of liquid detergents or a glass cleaner.

There are thousands of home brews, many of them quite potent. Instead of testing by the Food and Drug Administration, they are tested by time, developed and refined over decades, and sometimes altered in content or proportion or both. But there are no cautions on the labels, because there aren't any labels. So common sense must caution you against arbitrarily combining potentially potent ingredients such as ammonia and bleach. And since there are no skull and crossbones on home-remedy containers, it is not sensible to store these mixtures.

Here is a look at some of the most effective remedies, although they do not carry a money-back guarantee. And in many cases adjusting mix proportions may be necessary to get good results. For instance, on heavily mildewed wallboard, two cups of bleach per gallon of warm water may prove more effective than the standard recipe of one cup per gallon.

- Chalking Plaster Walls. To rescue old, powdering plaster walls, try washing them with a solution of one pint white household vinegar in one gallon of water. Repeated washings may be necessary to harden the surface sufficiently.

Roof leaks often leave stains with a dark outer ring. These asphalt traces can be hidden with pigmented white shellac before repainting.

- Deeply Stained Woods. Since liquids soak into the wood fibers of floors and furniture, it is often impossible to remove all traces of a dark stain. On floors, for instance, faint traces may remain even after sanding and refinishing. To hide a wood stain that cannot be removed, use chlorine bleach. Since different species of wood react to staining liquids and to bleach at different rates (surface finishes also affect the amount of color lightening), it is impossible to predict exactly how much bleach to use.

  Start by scrubbing the area with a solution of one part chlorine bleach to ten parts water, rinsing thoroughly and quickly after the application. The general effect is to remove all color—the stain and the tone of the wood—leaving a neutral, driftwood color that must be restained and resealed to blend in with surrounding areas.

- Dented Wood Furniture. When stains are set during an impact that dents the wood, clean or bleach, then try ironing out the dents. Cover the indentation with a wet blotter paper and press with a hot iron. Steaming the area should cause compressed wood fibers in the dent to swell close to their original size. Then seal and refinish the surface as desired.

- Flooded Wood Furniture. In minor floods or accidents with plumbing and heating systems, only an inch or so of water may cover the floor. But even a small flood hits wood furniture at its weak link—the very porous end grain of table and chair legs that soak up water like a sponge. To dry out wood saturated with water, set the legs in a container of kerosene. Depending on the degree of saturation, several days may be needed to drive out the water. Then the legs must be set in gasoline to drive out the kerosene.

  After this, the gasoline evaporates by itself, leaving dried wood that can be sanded, restained, and refinished. (Use flammable materials such as kerosene and gasoline with utmost caution.)

- Dirty, Greasy, or Fogging Glass. Remove built-up grease and grime by rubbing glass with a soft cloth dipped in kerosene or denatured alcohol and polish with tissue paper (the type used to wrap gifts) or even a crumpled newspaper. Among the many substitutes for proprietary glass cleaners are plain warm water; ¼ cup white vinegar in a quart of water; ⅛ cup alcohol in a quart of water (for cleaning in cold weather); one tablespoon of ammonia in a quart of water. To prevent glass from fogging, wipe the clean window with a soft cloth lightly coated with glycerine.

- Grease Spots on Wallpaper. Cover the spot with blotter paper and press with a warm iron. As grease is absorbed move the blotter so a fresh section covers the stain and press again.
- Discolored Tile Grout. Add enough bleach to a scouring powder (the powder may not contain any ammonia, which is dangerous in combination with bleach) to make a cleaning paste. Scrub it on dirty grout with a brush, then rinse. To remove stubborn dark stains in grout, try leaving a small amount of the cleaning paste on the spot, as a kind of poultice, covered with plastic wrap to keep in moisture. Remove the next day and continue the cleaning procedure. (To protect grout in high-moisture areas after cleaning, paint on a coat of liquid silicone.)
- Rust Stains on Bath Fixtures. Scrub with a mixture of lemon juice and salt. On stubborn stains, try an overnight poultice of lemon juice and baking soda to pull out the stain. On fiberglass fixtures (the molded, one-piece tubs and showers), where using abrasive cleaners would destroy the surface finish, try an overnight poultice of baking soda and water. To clean rust from marble tile or counters, wash with a 5 percent solution of oxalic acid or with lemon juice.
- Dirty Stainless Steel. Warm water and soap can handle all cleaning tasks, with a dash of ammonia to increase the surface luster (only a teaspoonful to about a quart of soapy water). Avoid abrasives other than an extremely fine polishing powder called feldspar (used in proprietary cleaners). It is wise to test even this pastelike abrasive on a small spot to be sure it won't cause graining and dull the finish.

JUST ASK

Q Is there any way to remove mildew spots that have started to appear through wallpaper?

A There's no easy way. In fact, the National Decorating Products Association says that once mildew appears, "it's usually too late to do anything but start all over"—which means stripping the paper, washing the wall, sizing, and repapering. Most common on vinyl and other non-porous wall coverings, mildew generally stems from the moisture in the wall-covering adhesive that is trapped under the covering. Special quick-drying vinyl adhesives solve this problem.

However, if the mildew spots are concentrated in a vertical strip about a foot wide, "sweating" pipes in the wall cavity could be causing the problem. While breaking open the wall to insulate the pipes would be impractical, it may be possible to drill a series of small holes through the framing members at the top and bottom of the wall to let the moisture escape.

Drilling through baseboard and ceiling trim in baths and kitchens would likely do more harm than good. But if the wall frame is accessible (through an exposed attic floor or open beams in an unfinished basement or crawl space) four or five ½-inch holes top and bottom could help.

Note that this is a particularly nifty way to bring a bit of heat into a pipe-filled wall cavity on an exterior wall where the pipes are subject to freezing. A few holes through the "shoe," a 2-by-4-inch timber nailed flat to the floor on which the wall studs rest, may let just enough warm air from a heated cellar into the otherwise inaccessible wall cavity.

3

PLUMBING REPAIRS
Solutions to Common Problems

Most parts of a residential plumbing system are out of sight and inaccessible, buried in the walls and floors. Before the framing is covered over, plumbers conduct a water test, literally filling up every pipe in the system, including vents, to test for leaks. Occasionally, part of the hidden system can break, for example, when cold weather freezes water in a supply pipe located in an exterior wall. But most plumbing problems are out in the open, in the fixtures.

Fixture Condensation

On hot and muggy summer days porcelain bathroom fixtures can deposit as much water on the floor inside as a summer shower deposits on the lawn outside. But what may look like a leak is probably condensation. And it can cause all kinds of problems.

For instance, a near-constant flow of condensate fosters mildew growth and accompanying bad odors, erodes grout between floor

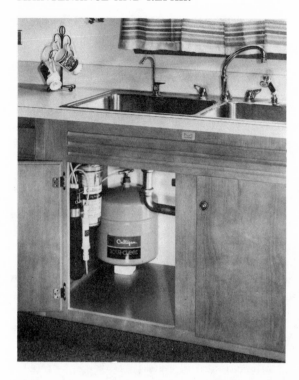

Water-conditioning equipment, such as this Culligan reverse osmosis system for drinking water, may be compact enough to fit under the sink.

tiles, breaks the adhesive bond between tiles and subflooring, and even delaminates plywood subfloors so that tile ripples up and down like the floor in a fun house. Unchecked, condensation can deteriorate every surface in the bathroom except the porcelain fixtures (particularly the toilet tank) that cause the problem.

Because the tank holds cool or even cold water, the tank surface temperature is well below the room air temperature. That difference makes the tank act like a weather front, where a line of warm air meeting cold air produces rain. You can solve the problem by dealing with the symptoms (the "rain") or the cause.

Coating all grouted floor tile seams with liquid silicone can help resist deterioration, although you still have to mop up the water. To keep the condensate from getting to the floor, a shallow catch basin can be fitted just beneath the tank. This slightly clunky-looking sheet metal or plastic pan (available in many hardware stores) funnels the collected condensate through a small tube into the bowl.

Cooling the bathroom air can eliminate the cause of the problem by equalizing temperatures on both sides of the tank. But central air-conditioning is expensive and, in some homes, impractical to install. A crafty way to get the same result is to insulate the tank. First, turn off the cold-water inlet; empty the tank and let it dry. Then glue a layer of foam rubber (½-inch thickness should be enough) around the inside of the tank.

It may seem a little weird, but it works. The foam remains intact even when submerged and reduces temperature transfer through the tank wall. Since the tank wall stays close to room temperature, moisture in the air will not condense on its surface.

Water Hammer

It's not hobgoblins going bump in the night; it's the plumbing. The phrase "water hammer" describes a range of sounds, from gentle clicking caused by cool pipes heating up, to alarmingly loud banging. Generally, even raucous water hammering is not dangerous or immediately damaging to the pipes. (What it does to your peace of mind is another matter.) In time, however, severe hammering can weaken fittings and eventually break apart soldered joints.

The problem is commonly caused when a flow of pressurized water is stopped abruptly, for instance, when an automatic solenoid valve in a clothes washer closes or when a single-lever mixing valve for a shower "jumps" from hot to cold. The solid tube of water literally bangs to a halt in the pipe, sometimes producing even more noise as the pipe, in turn, bangs against an adjacent wall stud. In some cases, worn washers at faucets allow air to be siphoned into the ends of supply pipes when the water is turned off, compounding the problem.

Water hammering can be solved by building a cushion into the supply line. The idea is analogous to inserting a shock absorber between the wheel and chassis of a car. It may not eliminate the potholes, but it can minimize their effect. In fact, one type of antihammer device is called a shock absorber.

The most basic cushion consists of a short length of pipe (usually 12–18 inches is long enough), mounted vertically, as an extension to some part of the supply line. It's like a vertical dead end filled with air that absorbs at least some of the hammering shock. Here's an example. A supply pipe for an outdoor spigot runs vertically up the wall to an elbow, where it turns 90 degrees to exit the house. That elbow fitting would be replaced with a T-fitting, feeding the spigot and the new air cushion pipe.

More sophisticated antihammer devices incorporate some type of bellows inside a fluid or gas-filled chamber—a true shock absorber. These stubby-shaped units take up much less room than pipe extensions and are more effective. But depending on the severity of the hammering, you may need only one unit, or one mounted just before the valve or faucet on several plumbing fixtures in the kitchen, bath, and laundry room.

Running Toilet Tanks

Nearly half the water used in average households flows through the toilet tank. The mechanism controlling the flow is out of sight and consequently out of mind. But it has many moving parts: an inlet valve and an outlet drain that open and close and several mechanical connections, all of which must work underwater.

Normal use causes only moderate deterioration, although in homes using private well water, mineral deposits are likely to accelerate the process. Unless the mechanism inside works properly, water can leak into the bowl twenty-four hours a day. That's wasteful if you are on the municipal water system and very expensive if you pump your own.

Although specific step-by-step procedures for replacement vary from one manufacturer to another, the innards of almost every type of toilet tank are now widely available in noncorroding plastic parts, blister packed complete with plastic connecting screws. The basic components include a rubber drain stopper (called the tank ball), a hollow ball and connecting arm to regulate water level, and the mechanism connected to that arm (called a float switch) that lets water into the tank.

The float switch is actually an automatic faucet, turned on and off as the hollow ball rises and falls with the water level in the tank. If bending the float arm down (to apply more pressure on the float switch as the tank fills) does not stop the flow, the switch is most likely worn or clogged. Water leaking past the rubber ball valve at the bottom of the tank can sometimes be stopped by carefully cleaning the connecting seam between the ball and the valve seat.

Short of complete replacement, minor leaking may be corrected by bending the float arm down a bit, by replacing the washer in the float switch, or by scraping away any scaly mineral deposits in the float switch. But if one of the main components must be replaced, it makes sense to upgrade the entire mechanism, possibly with a float-cup system that can reduce hissing and bubbling noises as the tank fills.

Running Faucets

In many older homes, classic star-shaped, porcelain inlaid, or wonderfully bulbous brass stem faucets have been replaced unnecessarily by more modern washerless faucets. These are somewhat more reliable than stem faucets but often a glaring contradiction to the ample and curvaceous style of older sinks and tubs.

However, the drip, drip, drip, from a worn stem faucet is certainly annoying and can be costly, as well. A kitchen and bathroom faucet dripping hot water wastes about 750 gallons a year—ten to fifteen full loads from the water heater straight down the drain.

All stem faucets, though not standardized from one manufacturer to another, operate as a threaded stem inside the faucet housing is screwed up and down to control water flow. The stem has three basic components: a seat washer at the bottom of the stem that closes against a valve seat on the faucet housing to shut off the water flow; a packing washer near the top of the stem that prevents water from leaking out the top of the faucet through the handle; and the stem section itself, which can be unscrewed and removed from the faucet. Sometimes just getting at the stem is the hardest part of the repair job.

Most old faucets secure the handle on the stem with a screw concealed beneath some type of decorative cap. The cap must be pried off carefully. Next (after turning off the water supply to the fixture), remove the screw and handle. If the screw slot is corroded, clean it with a thin knife or a hacksaw blade so that your screwdriver gets good leverage on the screw head. Once the slot is damaged, the handle can't be removed; on some models, the entire faucet must be replaced.

The next step is to unscrew the large packing nut, then the stem assembly beneath it. You can match the stem washers to identical types in a washer-selection package or simply take the stem to the hardware store when you buy replacements. Again, the screws holding the packing washer and seat washer in place may be corroded and difficult to remove without damaging the screw slot.

Work carefully. In some cases, particularly on faucets that are used a lot, even cleaning away scale and corrosion and replacing the washers may not completely stop the dripping. That's because the valve seat (the portion of the faucet housing the seat washer closes against) is worn. The same thing happens to brakes in a car. Generally, you can just replace the brake pads. But sometimes the drum or caliper the pads push against becomes warped or rough and must be resurfaced.

Most home centers and hardware stores sell seat-grinding kits containing a selection of guides and cutters that let you shave off the rough spots on the valve seat. These tools are generally turned by hand and controlled through guides that screw into the faucet. The resurfacing creates a positive, continuous seal between the washer and seat.

Although this repair job may seem tedious, removing a pair of old-style hot and cold faucets can be even more difficult. (And authentic reproduction fittings are expensive.) To remove the faucets, you have to reach up underneath the sink, in between the supply and drain pipes and behind the basin itself, to unscrew nuts holding the faucet to the fixture. And that can be a very frustrating task, even with a specially shaped faucet wrench.

JUST ASK

Q We have cleaned and repainted the kitchen after a grease fire on the stove singed surrounding countertops and bubbled paint on nearby cabinets. But a distinctive smoky odor still lingers. How can we get rid of it?

A Cleaning and repainting should have done the job, but sometimes fresh air and time are the only solution. (Some of the home remedies I've heard about include leaving mothballs in the cabinets, or an open package of baking soda.) But covering any lingering by-products of the fire should have covered any remaining aroma, as well. This makes me think there may be a hidden piece of wood, say, the cabinet partition next to the stove, that was damaged and not repainted.

If you are certain all surfaces have been resealed, inquire about a product called Bad Air Sponge, made by Mateson Chemical Corp. (1025 E. Montgomery Ave., Philadelphia, PA 19125). This nontoxic vinyl stearate compound is sold in solid form and simply exposed in the affected area for eighteen to twenty-four hours. The company suggests an amount of 1 pound of material per 100 cubic feet of space.

The product may also prove useful after furnace puffbacks that deposit a highly aromatic, oily grit on wall, floor, and ceiling surfaces. Dry chemical cleaning sponges (also available from Mateson) are used to clear away fire debris, although thorough sanding (down to unaffected bare wood) should prove just as effective.

4

ELECTRICAL REPAIRS
Solutions to Common Problems

Replacing a Light Switch

Making repairs and improvements in electrical systems calls for caution and common sense. You probably don't need the obligatory warning about unplugging appliances before working on them, unscrewing fuses, and tripping circuit breakers before working on circuit wiring. Most consumers rate electrical projects right at the bottom of the list of do-it-yourself work, partly because wiring is complicated, partly because, unlike jobs such as painting and papering, electrical work is unforgiving and potentially dangerous.

When a switch fails to activate a light fixture, you'll check the bulb first. But because switches have moving parts (unlike the bulk of a wiring system), they can break, too. However, before working on the switch, check the other end of the line at the fuse or breaker box to see if there is power in the circuit. At every step,

Audiolite's sound-activated switch, with adjustable sensitivity, provides a new kind of remote control over lamps and other appliances.

try to double-check your diagnosis. For example, by testing the bulb in another fixture that is receiving power. If it still does not light, you confirm the diagnosis of a bad bulb.

After removing the appropriate fuse or tripping the breaker, remove the switch cover plate. If you have any doubts about which circuit is controlled by the breaker you just tripped, check the switch with a neon voltage tester (a small, inexpensive device with two wire leads and a test lamp).

Whatever type of switch you select, make sure it is compatible with the wiring. (You may want to replace existing switches to have a more modern or special function switch, such as a dimmer, a silent switch with no on-off click, or a switch at the head of a stairs incorporating a small pilot lamp. This makes it easier and safer to locate in the dark.)

But switches that look the same on the surface may be quite different when you get a closer look inside the box. For instance, a single-pole switch that controls a fixture from just one location will most likely have three screw terminals: two for the power circuit and one for the ground wire. (Older homes may have a different ground system.) But what's called a three-way switch (two of them can be used to control one fixture from two different locations) will have three screw terminals plus the ground.

On older homes, be careful not to twist or bend the wires excessively. This can split brittle insulation covering the wire and even break the wire itself. To make a secure and safe connection, wrap the wire lead clockwise, three-quarters of the way around the terminal screw before tightening. When using solid (as opposed to stranded) wiring, take advantage of the provision on some switches for back wiring. With this safe and simple method, the wire leads are stripped of insulation, then simply pushed into holes in the back of the switch. A clamping mechanism inside secures the connections.

Fixing a Faulty Plug

Everyone knows that you are supposed to pull on the plug itself, not the wire connected to it, when removing a plug from an outlet. Everyone knows it, but somehow wires still become disconnected from the prongs that capture power from outlets in the wall.

To confirm that the fault is in the cord and plug and not in the wall outlet, first be sure that the outlet is "hot" by checking with a neon voltage tester. Also, be sure that the prongs of the plug are gripped by the outlet. If you feel little or no resistance, the mechanism inside may have been damaged or have lost its tension. In either case, the outlet (technically called a receptacle) should be replaced.

When the plug is damaged, the easiest solution is to snip it off and insert the raw ends of the wire into a quick-connect plug. These devices typically include some type of system that automatically pierces the wire insulation as the plug is installed. But the resulting electrical connections are tenuous. Also, this type of plug is probably the least resistant to strain caused by someone pulling the wire instead of the plug. And if that's what caused the problem initially, it may be likely to happen again.

Although it takes longer, it is safer to install a plug with screw or clamp terminals just like an outlet or switch or to replace the entire wire and plug, making new connections at the other end of the cord, inside a lamp base, for example.

Since there are many types and sizes of plugs, it is important to select a compatible replacement, for example, a three-pronged plug to fit a grounded receptacle. After threading the wire through the plug, it is good practice to tie what's known as an Underwriter's knot (as in Underwriters Laboratories). This secures the cord inside the plug and relieves strain if the cord is pulled.

In the UL knot the wire leads are separated, formed into a loop, then locked by snaking each lead through the loop made by the adjacent wire. Be sure to leave enough wire beyond the knot to reach the plug terminal screws. On thicker wiring, such as heavily insulated, grounded extension cords for power tools, strain relief is provided by a clamp built into the neck of heavy-duty plugs.

Adding Outlets

Few homes have electrical outlets in all the right places. Residential wiring systems tend to distribute power evenly, with the exception of special lines for high-capacity electric appliances such as a refrigerator and range. But most people do not divvy up their appliances based on the allocation of wall outlets provided by the electrician.

Bathroom outlets, for instance, may be needed for an electric shaver, a hair dryer, maybe an electric toothbrush. Few if any outlets are needed in a narrow hallway. But in a kitchen there may be countless appliances competing for limited outlet space. Even within rooms electrical demand is not spaced at equal intervals around the perimeter but concentrated in one spot, for instance, where home-entertainment equipment is grouped.

Adding outlets lets you customize the home wiring plan, cuts down on the number of extension cords, and cleans up the tangle of wires and adapter plugs behind groups of appliances. But increasing the number of outlets does not increase electrical capacity. Even running a new circuit from the fuse box cannot generate more electrical power in the house. If power used by four appliances attached through extension cords to a duplex receptacle (an outlet with space for two plugs) causes the circuit breaker to trip, rearranging the plugs in two duplex receptacles with the same power supply won't solve the problem.

To double up outlets, turn off power, remove the cover plate, and carefully pull out the existing receptacle. Since most outlet boxes are attached to wall studs, plan to enlarge the wall opening, working away from the stud. Remove what would be the common wall between the two outlet boxes; then tighten the two sections together with screws provided in the outlet box.

To transfer power from the existing receptacle to the new outlet, install short lengths of wire, called jumpers, between corresponding terminals. This task is greatly simplified on receptacles equipped for back wiring. In this case a guide right on the receptacle shows how much insulation to strip off the jumper wires, which can be inserted into slots instead of wrapped around conventional terminal screws.

On three-wire, grounded systems make sure to attach a green jumper wire to extend grounding protection to the new outlet. Older, two-prong systems can be replaced with three-prong, grounded receptacles, but only if the outlet box in the wall is grounded. In bathrooms and other areas where there is a risk from using electrical appliances near water, you can get extra protection by installing a special receptacle called a ground-fault circuit interrupter. This device combines a nearly instantaneous reacting circuit breaker and outlet in one unit to eliminate hazards from electrical shock.

In some cases it may be necessary to run new wires in the wall between outlets. You can use the spaces between framing members or use a surface system where codes permit. (With surface wiring, cable is run behind narrow, surface-mounted strips, called raceways.) Wiring is added to new homes before the walls are closed in. Even then, the electrician must drill through wall studs to run cable around a room and through layers of framing to run wires from floor to floor. This job is complicated by all the other materials sharing space between wall studs and rafters with the wiring—plumbing pipes and insulation, for example.

You can imagine how much harder it is to run new wires when the wall cavities are covered. The task is called fishing wires. And it requires a fisherman's patience. Suppose you want to bring a new cable from the main panel on the first floor up to a new workroom in the attic. The solution is to find a hidden path through the guts of the house. When a concealed space is boxed in by framing, you may have to break through a small section of wall in order to drill through a sill, for example. To snake wires through the hole, insert a fish tape (a flat piece of spring metal with a small hook on the end) from each side of the hole. The idea is to connect the hooks by touch and pull one fish tape through, and the new electrical cable along with it.

A Silent Doorbell

Doorbells are not part of the standard home-wiring system. They use less power through thinner wires and a "step-down" transformer. And unlike house wiring that may shoot sparks and blow fuses when there is a problem, bell systems usually just stop working. A bell system can stay intact but inoperative for years.

Procrastinating do-it-yourselfers may not be happy to learn how easy it is to diagnose faults in a bell system. To start with, remove the push button and touch a screwdriver across the electrical contacts. (This is an unsafe procedure on higher-powered house wiring.) If this makes the bell sound, the push button is defective—a common problem, since the button is the system's principal working part.

Unless there is a break in the bell wire, replacing either the transformer or the bell unit will fix the system. If crossing the button contacts does not make the bell sound, check for power with a neon voltage tester at the transformer. If it is producing power, replace the bell unit. If there is no power output, replace the transformer.

JUST ASK

Q Water emptying from the downspout has eroded a shallow trench next to the foundation. The cellar isn't wet yet, but I'm afraid it may be if this continues. How can I solve the problem without digging up the bushes and laying underground pipe?

A If the downspout in question is on the low side of the house (water emptying from it runs away from, not back to, the building), the solution is simple. Pop rivet or screw an elbow fitting to the end of the downspout. Water can be directed from the elbow into a short length of drainpipe leading away from the house or onto a masonry splash block that spreads the flow onto the ground or into a diffuser. These devices are like perforated hoses that extend into the yard a few feet and dribble the water onto the ground to reduce erosion.

Also, fill in the existing gully along the house with compacted soil. Try to create a slight slope away from the foundation to encourage drainage. Any of these systems (even the elbow extension by itself) will work on the low side of a sloped site.

On the high side of the house, where water from the gutter will run back to the foundation, there is no good substitute for the underground drains you don't want to dig. Of course, the drainpipe could be laid above grade, behind the bushes, as long as it sloped a bit to encourage drainage around the house to a point where it can be released without flowing back toward the building. Another possibility is to slope a short length of underground pipe out into the yard and into a dry well (a sunken pit filled with rock that acts as a catch basin). But that will require at least as much excavation as the foundation pipes.

NOVEMBER

1 MORE AND MORE INSULATION:
It's Not Always the Energy-Saving Answer

Adding insulation is one way to cut fuel bills. Although it is probably the most publicized, it is only one part of a sensible, cost-efficient, energy-saving program. And if energy saving seems a tired phrase when ample oil supplies have leaders of oil-exporting nations bicker-

2 ENGINEERING A FALL TUNE-UP:
One for the Car and One for the Furnace

Remember the last time your car got stuck during a winter storm? Maybe the battery quit, or a finicky ignition system lost its spark in the cold. Marooned in a dead car, you have time to contemplate the foolishness of postponing the tune-up you were going to get before

3 RAISING THE ROOFING QUESTION:
Recognizing Signs of Decay and Singling Out the Proper Shingles

As winter approaches, homeowners need to be sure that the roof will last through another season of ice and snow without leaking. But too often a hurried decision about repairing or replacing a roof is prompted by the sudden appearance of dark, dripping blotches in the

4 DIAGNOSING REPAIRS:
Discovering What's Wrong Is Half the Battle

Home repair and maintenance, the deadly duo, is an inevitable and not terribly exciting part of owning or renting a place to live. It doesn't matter where the home is or how big and expensive it is; every building deteriorates in time, inside and out. But by recognizing the

Preparing for Winter

ing among themselves instead of dictating terms to the world, remember that saving energy means saving money. But every fall, home consumers hear the insulation hard sell again: Add another layer in the attic, in the crawl space. The heavy-handed message is that more is always better and that much more is much better. But it ain't necessarily so.

the weather changed. It pays to remember that a home-heating plant needs the same kind of tune-up. Most furnaces are very much like cars. A typical oil-fired system, for instance, has a fuel tank, a fuel line and filters, a carburetion system, ignition points, timing controls, a fan, belts, a fuse, wiring, temperature gauges, a combustion chamber, even an exhaust pipe. And like your car, the furnace will work more safely and efficiently after a seasonal tune-up.

ceiling. Although a typical residential roof is architecturally unexciting and represents only about 5 percent of total construction costs, it is a crucial construction component—the first line of defense against water, which, aside from fire, has the most damaging effect on buildings.

signs of trouble with everything from roof shingles to foundation blocks and diagnosing problems early on, damage can be limited and repair costs minimized. Left unattended, deterioration will spread, often growing exponentially along with the time and money required for repair.

1

MORE AND MORE INSULATION
It's Not Always the Energy-Saving Answer

Adding insulation is one way to cut fuel bills. Although it is probably the most publicized, it is only one part of a sensible, cost-efficient, energy-saving program. And if energy saving seems a tired phrase when ample oil supplies have leaders of oil-exporting nations bickering among themselves instead of dictating terms to the world, remember that saving energy means saving money.

Every fall, home consumers hear the insulation hard sell: Add another layer in the attic, in the crawl space, in the common wall to the garage; and if those are filled to the brim, find another spot. The heavy-handed message is that more is always better and that much more is much better.

That's true for an old building with no insulation in the walls. It's not true for other buildings, old or new, already protected to code standards. But the insulation manufacturers are not dead wrong, just overstating their case and glossing over the way insulation provides thermal protection—according to the principle of diminishing returns.

The first inch in the wall offers the greatest benefit, a dramatic annual reduction in fuel bills for a modest one-time investment. The second inch is a very good buy; the third, only a good buy. And so it goes, mirroring the acceleration curve of a car, which is graphically displayed as a nearly vertical line in first gear, an increasing curve through second and third, and a tapped-out, nearly horizontal line in fourth.

If there was enough room, it would be reasonable to add inch after inch, even though each one offered less and less benefit, if the cost of each layer was reduced in proportion to the energy it saved. But every inch costs the same. That makes the last inch of the extra layer of six-inch batting in the attic floor a terrible investment.

None of this makes common sense when practical experience demonstrates that two sweaters are warmer than one and that a big, puffy down jacket insulates better than a thin jacket with a quilted surface and sewn-through seams. But more is not necessarily better.

The insulation material itself, whether fiberglass or cellulose or foam base, applied as loose fill or batts or rigid panels, does not retain heat. Dead air trapped in the material provides the thermal resistance. That's why insulation is lightweight like down feath-

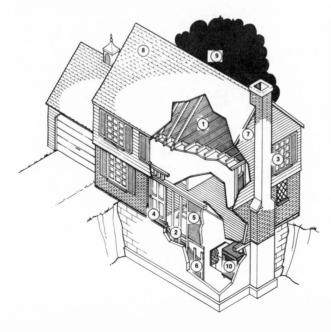

To provide a fully insulated "envelope" around the living space, insulation is needed on foundation and upper walls, and attic floor.

ers, why it loses effectiveness when compressed, why condensation soaking through insulating material and the air spaces causes heat loss in addition to mold and mildew. A down jacket is great in the cold but not in a wet snow or rain.

A quilted down jacket models some of the problems with insulating insulation. Sewn-through seams act like wall studs in a building linking exterior and interior surfaces. Examine better-made down gear and you will see that sewn-through seams are replaced with material baffles. The highest-quality mountaineering parkas are often designed as two baffled jackets in one, arranged so quilted pouches on the outer shell cover the seams on the inner shell. Connections are cold. Disconnections are warm.

Although it's difficult to know how much dead air is trapped in a building material, weight is a good indicator. Imagine a house with walls of steel, which is rolled during fabrication specifically to eliminate trapped air bubbles that would reduce its strength. Adding layer after layer of steel wouldn't help, either. Cold temperatures would take longer to get through, but eventually it would be just about as frigid inside as outside.

Thinking of insulation as a vehicle for trapped air helps to explain why softwood log cabins may not last as long as hardwood cabins but are easier to keep warm (softwood is lighter, with more space between wood fibers); why large, single-thickness picture windows can make a room chilly and double-glass sandwiching a layer of dead air makes so much difference. The vehicle is always the weak link, whether it's bits of cellulose or minute contact points between spun-glass fibers. So why not dispense with the vehicle altogether and leave wall cavities full of dead air and nothing else?

At the risk of overstating the case against more and more insulation, it should be noted that old, uninsulated frame houses with a full four inches of relatively dead air in the walls didn't have problems with condensation. Exterior paint didn't peel as much or as often as it does on tightly sealed houses. Windows were single thickness and still didn't fog up. Fireplaces and furnaces didn't need special inlet ducts to provide air to support combustion, as is required in superinsulated homes. And wooden studs and sills were less likely to rot. Of course, fuel was cheap, and more heat was more expedient than more insulation.

A thorough, careful installation of a modest amount of insulation is generally less expensive and more energy efficient than the advertised insulation overdose. On new construction or renovations where the walls are opened, this means stapling folded edges of insulating batts against wood studs without gaps. In cold climates where 2-by-6 construction may be suggested to allow more room for insulation, consider rigid styrene board sheathing on conventional 2-by-4 framing instead. Expanded polystyrene has nearly double the R value (thermal resistance) per inch of fiberglass batts and covers the wood frame to reduce any sewn-through-seam effect.

As fall turns to winter, you'll read more about insulation, because years of oversimplified publicity have practically obliterated a sensible, whole-house approach to saving energy and reducing winter fuel bills.

For more information, although it will almost certainly contradict the point of view above, truckloads of data are available from the major manufacturers (Certain Teed, Owens-Corning, and others). Also, check any of the how-to magazines for pages of ads with information offers.

Possibly the most interesting array of material on the subject available from many government sources is provided by the Conservation and Renewable Energy Inquiry and Referral Service branch of the Department of Energy. It can provide lists of books, recent articles, consumer pamphlets, technical reports, and more. A great source! Write to CAREIRS, Box 8900, Silver Spring, MD 20907.

JUST ASK

Q I have large triangular vents at each end of my attic. I know they help to cool the attic in summer, but shouldn't I close them off to save heat in winter?

A Common sense says yes, close them the way you close a window against winter wind. But energy systems in a house are often nonsensical. Here's why you should leave them at least partially open.

On a freezing but clear winter day the sun will bake asphalt roof shingles and heat the attic. Temperatures won't match summer hotbox conditions, but the space could easily reach 100° F. If the vents are closed, any moisture in the warm, stagnant air (and normal activity will produce plenty of moisture) will condense at night, when temperatures in the unheated attic drop drastically. Several days of this hot-cold cycle can produce enough water to resemble a severe roof leak, particularly when attic floors do not contain a vapor barrier.

One rule of thumb for attics with floor insulation and a vapor barrier is 1 square foot of vent inlet and outlet per 600 square feet of ceiling area. At least half the vent total should be placed where the roof peak meets the end walls of the house, normally with triangular gable-end vents. The other half can be distributed along the roof overhangs, normally with round-plug or strip-grill eave vents.

2

ENGINEERING A FALL TUNE-UP

One for the Car and One for the Furnace

Remember the last time your car got stuck during a winter storm? Maybe the battery quit, or a finicky ignition system lost its spark in the cold. Marooned in a dead car with the snow beginning to drift, even friendly local streets can seem like frozen, uninhabited tundra, a lonely place to contemplate the foolishness of postponing the tune-up you were going to get before the weather changed.

Most consumers remember to prepare a car for winter because it is a tangible consumer product. It requires fuel on a regular basis, new tires, oil, filters, and all sorts of regular maintenance. It can be difficult to remember that a home-heating plant needs the same preparation. Too often consumers think of the furnace as one more static part of the house, requiring the same attention as foundations and fuse boxes, i.e., none at all until something breaks.

But most furnaces are very much like cars. A typical oil-fired system, for instance, has a fuel tank, fuel line and filters, a carburetion system, ignition points, timing controls, a fan, belts, a fuse,

*An oil furnace needs
an annual tune-up of
basic cleaning and
checks on the exhaust
and ignition systems
to stay safe and
energy efficient.*

wiring, temperature gauges, a combustion chamber, even an exhaust pipe.

Now think of a car untuned since October 1985, sitting in the driveway for the last four or five months, unused just like a furnace. Consider what might happen when the ignition key is turned: quite possibly nothing at all. Most furnaces don't reflect lack of maintenance or use this dramatically. They'll chug into action but run inefficiently at best, and dangerously at worst.

A seasonal tune-up is the answer. Most owner's manuals limit consumer involvement to changing air filters; furnace manufacturers purposely shortcut maintenance and troubleshooting information with the inevitable line: Call an authorized dealer.

That's certainly a reasonable suggestion. Imprecise maintenance language could lead to incorrect, potentially dangerous adjustments. Manufacturers may limit maintenance information to limit their liability. That doesn't mean basic furnace maintenance is too time-consuming or too technical for owners to handle.

I am not a furnace technician, yet in about an hour I get through basic cleaning, checking blower-belt tension, pulling the electrodes from the combustion chamber, cleaning them, checking the gap and other details, all without special tools or equipment. This maintenance is a distinct level above changing filters. But it's not much more complicated than wiring an outlet, once you know the sequence of events, which you can get from how-to books and service manuals, available from some manufacturers. Or you can pick up the same details by hovering over the professional who does the work for a few years, until it dawns on you that he's in and out in forty-five minutes—and you could be, too.

A full-service call, the kind of maintenance that should be done every few years even if you do a good job yourself, involves a really complete look at the furnace system. Professionals should not only clean blowers, fans, and grills but adjust the rate of combustion and analyze furnace operation with a series of instruments well beyond the scope of do-it-yourselfers. Here are the highlights that should be covered in a full-blown professional service call.

- For Oil Burners. Annual servicing is recommended. Burner-motor air intakes are cleaned. Motors, where required, are lubricated. The air-to-oil mix is adjusted. Electrode igniters are removed from the firebox, and cleaned and checked for proper gap. The oil-spray nozzle is unscrewed, cleaned in solvent, and any grit is blown clear with compressed air. The heat exchanger, firebox, exhaust stack, and chimney-soot dump are checked for oil-laden soot accumulations—a sign of incomplete combustion and a potential fire hazard. The photoelectric cell is cleaned. On older systems with a stack relay mounted in a metal exhaust duct between furnace and chimney, the relay box is removed, and the heat-sensing element protruding into the stack is cleaned. The filter in oil-supply lines should be checked, particularly if the furnace was used immediately after an oil delivery or when the oil level in the tank was very low. In both cases, sludge and grit at the bottom of the tank may have been carried into the line. Finally, instruments are used to measure flue temperature, the draft rate, smoke density (called the smoke spot number), and CO_2 levels in flue gases.
- For Gas Burners. Full servicing is recommended every two or three years. Because gas burns cleanly, maintenance on gas burners is minimal. Air-intake grills are cleaned. The gas-to-air mix is adjusted. The pilot light is cleaned and adjusted to activate the thermocouple. This device, often the weak link in a gas furnace, converts pilot-light heat to the electricity, which is used by a solenoid valve to keep the main gas supply valve open. If the pilot is extinguished, the thermocouple stops pro-

ducing electricity, the solenoid lets go, and the gas flow ceases. The holes (called jets) in gas spuds (small knobs that feed gas from a main supply manifold to the burner) are cleaned with a thin, soft wire.

Remember that general guidelines, though they may seem very explicit, are always superseded by manufacturers' instructions, which do vary. Also, you must follow safety rules (cutting off the electric supply, for instance) and your common sense. If you feel uneasy or unsure about following service-manual sequences, trust your feelings. Hire a professional and use some of the information above to make sure you get a full-service service call.

Arranging for seasonal, start-up maintenance on home-heating plants does not require a lot of comparison shopping. Unlike energy-saving retrofits, where an array of exotic products and services is available, heating maintenance is a straightforward job.

It can be performed by a plumbing and heating contractor, by the manufacturer's personnel, or local contractors fulfilling the manufacturer's service agreement, and sometimes by selected contractors as a follow-up service to a utility company's energy audit. Most oil and gas companies employ service staff to care for the equipment they supply with fuel. If your utility does not supply service, chances are it will be able to recommend a reliable service contractor. Don't forget to call a chimney sweep and include woodburning stoves and their flues in the cleaning and service regimen.

JUST ASK

Q I'm getting conflicting opinions about the best material to use for an exposed wood deck that must be able to survive our sometimes severe winters. Should it be treated wood or construction-grade wood with a sealer?

A I have built construction-grade decks (untreated) in northern New Hampshire that are intact and not rotted out fifteen years later. And they sit under a lot of snow most of the winter. But much of the credit is due to conscientious clients who followed the advice of resealing the deck every fall.

I applied two coats of clear, penetrating sealer (a product that included pentachlorophenol, now banned), then left the remains of a five-gallon can and a roller for the homeowner. Now the fir is silvery gray, checked (surface openings of the grain that often appear to be splits but aren't), and quite solid.

So if you can remember to reseal the deck annually (or even every other year), even a mediocre wood specie and grade will last. If this sounds like the perennial bottom line on your to-do list, pressure-treated timber may be a better choice. Wood-preserving chemicals are forced into the wood in a giant pressure cooker so that the grain is protected inside and out. Pressure-treated timbers are the best choice for ledgers (part of the frame nailed to the existing house, for example) where water is likely to run and collect and where sunlight and ventilation will be minimal.

If the typically green hue left by the treatment is bothersome, try altering it with a semitransparent, penetrating wood stain. If you hide the tone with paint, you'll be out there every few years scraping and repainting, which is a whole lot worse than slopping on another layer of clear sealer.

3

RAISING THE ROOFING QUESTION

Recognizing Signs of Decay and Singling Out the Proper Shingles

As winter approaches, homeowners need to be sure that the roof will last through another season of ice and snow without leaking. But too often a hurried decision about repairing or replacing a roof is prompted by the sudden appearance of dark, dripping blotches in the ceiling.

It's easy to forget about the roof, which is hidden behind a facade on many buildings and is not as prominent or interesting as the windows, doors, and siding at eye level. Although a typical residential roof is architecturally unexciting and represents only about 5 percent of total construction costs, it is a crucial construction component—the first line of defense against water, which, aside from fire, has the most damaging effect on buildings.

Most roofs (81 percent of residential buildings) are covered with asphalt shingles or continuous sheets known as roll roofing. (About 10 percent have wood roofs, while the remainder have tile, slate, and other specialties.) A typical shingle roof should last fifteen to twenty years, depending on a variety of environmental factors, such as wind and snow, and on shingle weight. (Roofing is priced by the "square" (100 square feet) and rated by weight. (A standard 240-pound rating indicates that enough shingles to cover one square will weigh 240 pounds.)

Shingle weight is an important factor on new roofs and on reroofing jobs where a layer of new shingles is laid directly over the existing roof. Heavier shingles last longer, carry a longer warranty, and may offer a better fire rating. Naturally, they are more expensive than lighter shingles. The heavyweight category is generally 300 pounds per square or more, often configured in layers simulating wood shakes.

Heavier shingles may be a good choice on a new home or addition but are usually a bad choice for reroofing. Rafters designed to hold one layer of shingles may be overloaded by heavyweight roofing, particularly when a second layer of shingles is covered by a third. (No more than three layers of light-to-medium-weight

Flat and low-slope roll roofs, particularly those with breaks for chimneys and skylights, are among the most difficult to seal and flash.

shingles should be applied even if beefy rafters could hold more, because it is not possible to nail the uppermost layer to a solid base.)

There is another Catch-22 to reroofing. Unless existing shingles are brittle or cracked or curling or missing surface granules, there is probably no need to reroof. But by the time shingles are brittle and curling, they do not make a satisfactory base for reroofing. Depressions where shingle tabs have broken off, and bulges where other tabs have curled, will be reflected in the new roof. Isolated problems can be repaired before reroofing. But when damage is widespread, spending extra money to have the old roof removed is a good investment that makes the new roof look better and last longer.

There are three clear signs of roof decay more subtle than a dripping ceiling.

1. Surface granules begin to wash off some of the shingles, accumulating in gutters and particularly where downspouts discharge rainwater onto the ground.
2. Bare spots, most noticeable when white granules uncover black asphalt, erode to expose nail heads holding the shingle in place. (Nails puncture the roof, providing an entry point for water.)
3. Continuous exposure to seasonal swings in humidity and temperature curls the tabs (the exposed section of the shingle). The outside edge curls down, while the middle raises up. As the inverted cupping action continues, stress builds until the tab cracks, then breaks free, exposing more nail heads to the weather.

The next big decision (on first-time and reroofing jobs) is whether to use asphalt or fiberglass shingles. That's the way the question is usually posed, even though the terminology is misleading. "Asphalt" and "fiberglass" shingles are both basically asphalt shingles. The difference is in the bottom layer of the shingle, called the base mat. In all-asphalt shingles, the mat and upper layers are asphalt. In fiberglass shingles, the mat is a synthetic fiberglass mesh that is lighter, stronger, and longer lasting than organic base mats.

Approximately 80 percent of all shingles sold now are fiberglass-mat, asphalt shingles. This configuration, introduced in 1978, is used in almost all heavyweight, overlay-type shingles, which generally carry a twenty-five-year warranty. (The average life span of a standard, 240-pound shingle roof is fifteen to twenty years, depending on site conditions.) All-asphalt shingles are now relegated to lighter weights and a smaller share of the market as the popularity of fiberglass-mat shingles continues to grow, particularly since the two types now cost about the same amount of money.

Choosing the shingle color (only the surface granules are colored) is a question of personal taste. However, the general consensus is that bold blues, greens, and reds become difficult to live with after a few seasons, if not sooner. White or light gray shingles help to make a house look larger, the way a white ceiling seems higher and a dark ceiling seems lower. From a practical point of view, white mars more easily than dark shingles and shows wear sooner. But white shingles reflect more sunlight than dark shingles, which keeps a house cooler (and reduces the air-conditioning load) in summer.

By now, most consumers know to comparison shop and solicit bids from several contractors, to check for a home-improvement license where required, for contractor's liability insurance and recommendations, and for potential black marks with the local Consumer Protection Agency and Better Business Bureau.

One unique twist of roofing contracts is your right to a double warranty. One is from the contractor. It covers the installation and generally ranges from two to five years, depending on climate and type of roof. The second warranty is from the manufacturer. It covers the shingles only, and for most products ranges from ten to twenty years. But even an ironclad material warranty is no defense against poor workmanship.

Aside from fiberglass mats, several large manufacturers have recently introduced another improvement—a shingle specially coated to resist the formation of mildew and fungus that prematurely ages a roof while turning it green. The system uses a porous zinc compound with a time-release fungicide agent that washes over the shingles when it rains. These shingles are designated "FRS" on the bundle wrapper and cost 5 to 10 percent more than shingles without the coating. They are well suited for roofs in hot, humid areas where one side of the roof is shaded from sunlight and sheltered from circulating air.

For a free, informative, well-illustrated booklet on asphalt-shingle selection and step-by-step application, write to the Asphalt Roofing Manufacturers Association, 6288 Montrose, Rockville, MD 20852. Request their publication entitled, "Good Application Makes a Good Roof Better."

JUST ASK

Q Is there any way to stop wallboard nails from "popping"? Several wallboard seams in our new house are developing little discolored bumps, which break the spackle as the nail head pushes through.

A You are experiencing a problem that is common in recently built wood-frame buildings, caused most often by lumber shrinkage. It's likely that if you do nothing now and wait for the heating season and the last of the nail head crop to bloom through wallboard joint compound, you'll have to make repairs only once, after the lumber has lost most of its excess moisture and stabilized.

But sometimes nail popping is caused when wallboard panels are not held tightly against the framing during nailing. Extra stresses created when nails are used to pull the wallboard into place encourage popping. In both cases, the most durable repair method is to remove the old nail, replace it with a drive screw (the choice of commercial wallboard installers), which has a sharp point, a Phillips head, and wide threads along the shank to prevent loosening.

Tighten the drive screw until it seats just slightly below the wallboard surface. Then cover with successive layers of joint compound. A 1¼-inch drive screw is recommended for ⅜-, ½-, and ⅝-inch thick wallboard.

4

DIAGNOSING REPAIRS

Discovering What's Wrong Is Half the Battle

Home repair and maintenance, the deadly duo, is an inevitable and not terribly exciting part of owning or renting a place to live. It doesn't matter where the home is or how big and expensive it is; every building deteriorates in time, inside and out. But by recognizing the signs of trouble with everything from roof shingles to foundation blocks and diagnosing problems early on, damage can be limited and repair costs minimized. Left unattended, deterioration will spread, often growing exponentially along with the time and money required for repair.

Does home diagnosis start to sound a lot like medical diagnosis? It should, because there are many similarities. Both require detective work, looking for clues in the circulatory/plumbing system, the nervous/electrical system, the respiratory/hot-air heating system, searching for weak links in the complex skeletal/framing system and into the depths of the gastrointestinal/drainage system.

Experience is the best diagnostic teacher; you see a minor foundation fault that leads to basement leaks on one job, and remember nailing up heavy, moisture-laden 2-by-4s that dis-

An experienced contractor can explain when it makes sense to save what's there and when it's more practical to tear away and rebuild.

rupted wallboard seams on another. Sometimes the cause and effect are subtly connected, separated by time or layers of building materials. That makes the detective work more challenging, and for many, more fun.

Not many homeowners and renters have years of experience on construction sites. But just as certain physical complaints of a patient can predict specific ailments and indicate a course of medical treatment, certain signs of damage in a building preview the type and extent of deterioration and indicate preventive measures and home repairs to solve the problem.

General diagnostic conclusions aren't always correct. Every building, even nearly identical row houses or high ranches, has its own peculiarities. But in most cases the following telltale indicators work despite differences in architectural style and construction. And they help inexperienced home consumers communicate with contractors by zeroing in on specific problems and solutions.

• Roofing. Asphalt shingles, the most common roofing material, display several warning signs before giving way. Watch for accumulations of small granules from the shingle surface in gutters and at downspout outlets where they are washed by the rain. As this top coating disappears, patches of asphalt will start to show, which is particularly noticeable on light-colored shingles.

In the next stage of deterioration, exposed shingles become brittle. Individual sections, called tabs, start to curl and may break away, leaving shingles and nails below open to the weather. When groups of shingles on the roof begin to curl, leaks are likely within the next several seasons. When tabs crack and break loose, leaks are imminent.

- Siding. On brick siding, mortar joints are the weak link. Watch for hairline cracks that grow across the full width of mortar, causing sections to loosen or fall out. Once small cracks open the mortar to the weather (water in particular), deterioration increases exponentially. Repointing, or scraping out the old mortar and adding fresh material, combined with a protective coating of clear silicone sealer on the entire wall solves the problem. (Note that clear masonry sealers will darken concrete, block, brick, and even most stone a shade or two but leave the natural texture and color gradations of the material intact.)

  On wooden siding, deterioration may start as twisting forces in the wooden building frame and in the siding itself work to disrupt joints and loosen nails. Clapboards and other individual boards (as opposed to sheets of plywood) may begin to crack under the stresses, usually starting near the end of the board where it is nailed. As with masonry, the trick is to spot the problem early, before water infiltrates the cracks to rot unprotected wood and, in winter, widen the split as the water freezes and expands. Renail and caulk exposed seams to keep the building skin intact. Where boards are badly twisted, try substituting wood screws for nails.

- Paint. Since a paint film is the outermost protective layer on a building, its condition often previews what is about to occur underneath. Alligatoring, one of the most common paint problems, which, in the final stages, produces a rectangular grid of cracks like an alligator's skin, generally starts as a series of short, thin lines running in one direction. More cracks appear, then branch out at right angles, making the grid pattern.

  The condition is most often caused when a finish coat of paint is applied before the prime coat has completely dried and when one very thick coat of paint is applied instead of two thinner coats. After scraping the surface, sand down edges of any remaining paint, prime the exposed wood, then repaint.

- Masonry Steps and Patios. Concrete steps, a masonry porch, a driveway, or a patio are almost always built independently of the building they are attached to. As a result, a common problem is cracking and separation between, say, the front steps and the house. The two structures simply settle and move in different directions.

  There is no glue strong enough to keep the pieces together once a crack develops and begins to widen. But in most cases the movement is relatively minor and eventually stabilizes. But until it does, other problems can develop as water runs into the crack, washes away soil supporting the steps, causing more settling, and seeps through foundation walls that may not have been waterproofed because they were protected by the steps.

  Once you spot the crack, scrape out any loose material, brush away any dirt or grainy residue, and fill the crack with silicone caulk, leaving some excess above the seam. Silicone is preferable to other caulks for this job, since it is highly resilient and will adhere to the house and to the steps as they continue to separate (only up to a point, of course). If the caulk breaks lose, pull out the old material and lay in a new, thicker bead.

- Foundations. Cracks and other problems in masonry foundations can be very worrisome to the people living above the fault lines. But in most cases foundation cracks are a result of surface tension and only skin-deep. To be sure, measure from the corner to locate the crack, then look for it inside on the basement or crawl-space wall. When the same pattern appears in the same place inside and out, there is a potentially serious structural fault. Typical "staircase cracking" following the mortar joints from top to bottom in concrete-block foundations, for instance, usually indicates that the foundation wall is heading in two different directions.

  But even when the cracking is skin-deep, further deterioration can be prevented by repointing. On the critical seam between the foundation and cellar floor, cracking may be followed by slow seepage in heavy rains, then by regular flooding with every rain. To catch that problem early, scrape out any loose mortar, make sure the crack is dry and clear of grainy debris, then force a stiff mixture of hydraulic cement into the crack. The hydraulic action causes the mix to swell slightly as it hardens, filling irregular crevices.

JUST ASK

Q I have an old house in which the plumbing pipes rattle when someone turns on the tap. How can I make sure this noise won't occur in the bathroom of our new addition?

A The secret is to isolate, as much as possible, the pipes from the frame. Ask at a plumbing-supply shop (a local hardware store or home center might not carry these items) for pipe spacers and insulators. These range from devices that look like curtain-rod hangers (mounted on wall studs but suspending the pipe in a plastic holder away from the stud) to molded foam spacers.

While the addition is still under construction (before the walls are covered), see if you can produce the banging and rattling by pushing on the pipes. If they move a bit but don't rattle now, you should have peace and quiet later on.

DECEMBER

1 HEADING OFF WATER DAMAGE:
Winter Snows Can Mean Big Trouble for Roofs and Foundations

Aside from fire, which can destroy a home in minutes, water causes the most long-term deterioration and damage to buildings. Roof shingles, gutters, downspouts, and foundation drains designed to carry

2 COPING WITH WINTER EMERGENCIES:
Specialized Gadgets to Help Prevent or Minimize Household Disasters

It's hard to appreciate how much you depend on electricity in a house or apartment until there's a power failure. In some homes a

3 FIGHTING OFF THE ELEMENTS:
Working Outside to Protect the Inside

Inside the house, cooking, washing, and the other operations of day-to-day living cause gradual deterioration. Outside, the elements cause decay, particularly water. It seems to find the smallest opening between roof shingles and flashing and soaks into unprotected wood,

4 IMPROVING THE EFFICIENCY OF WOOD-BURNING STOVES:
Catalytic Combustors Increase Heat Output, Reduce Pollutants

One small piece of equipment has revolutionized wood heating. Overlooked by many wood-stove manufacturers until this season, it

Dealing with Cold Weather

water away from the house all can become ineffective when winter weather turns free-flowing water into slush and ice.

blackout can cut off water, light, heat, and refrigeration, bringing even the most commonplace activities to a halt. But what might turn into a romantic adventure with candles, cold cuts, and tepid beer in the summer can be destructive, costly, and scary in the winter. The risk of a power failure, fire, or flood increases in winter when ice storms can bring down electrical lines, when wood and coal stoves can spit embers onto a rug, and when low temperatures can rupture plumbing pipes. Winter weather increases not only the risks but also the difficulty of coping with these emergencies in the cold and dark.

causing swelling, warping, and rot. Protecting the house against water damage on the outside goes a long way toward minimizing maintenance and repair work on the inside.

improves heat output while reducing exhaust pollutants and creosote buildup. Corning's catalytic combustor is a thick, honeycomb-shaped wafer through which smoke passes on its way to the chimney. Special coatings on the wafer spark a complex series of chemical changes in the smoke, "cracking it," as the Corning engineers explain the process, into particles that can be reburned. Early tests conducted by Corning and independent labs showed the use of a combustor led to a 20 percent increase in heat output, a 75 percent reduction in exhaust pollutants, and a 95 percent burn of creosote-producing gases.

1

HEADING OFF WATER DAMAGE

Winter Snows Can Mean Big Trouble for Roofs and Foundations

Aside from fire, which can destroy a home in minutes, water causes the most long-term deterioration and damage to buildings. Roof shingles, gutters, downspouts, and foundation drains designed to carry water away from the house are often ineffective when winter weather turns free-flowing water into slush and ice.

Working from top to bottom, here are several spots where minor repairs or improvements can prevent major damage from winter weather.

Flat and nearly flat roofs, which are common on row houses, are generally the most difficult to protect against damage, particularly if they are well insulated. Even though the house is warm inside, the temperature of the roof's surface is close to ground temperature. If snow sticks and builds to a foot or more in the driveway, it will be just as deep on the roof.

All structures are designed to support predictable snow loads. Weight is rarely the problem. But when the storm subsides and the sun shines, the snow begins to melt—especially the bottom inch or so just above the roof, which absorbs heat from the sun's rays and is shielded from cold air and wind by the blanket of snow above.

Wire baskets and other leaf guards designed to keep drain inlets clear can encourage the formation of ice dams if even a few leaves or twigs are trapped at the drain entrance. It may seem like overkill, but it is a good idea to check all drains on the roof, including connections between gutters and downspouts, and even to sweep the roof completely clean of debris. Otherwise, leaf guards and wire baskets may act as barriers. Melted snow that turns to slush, then to ice as the sun goes down and temperatures drop, starts to accumulate on the roof and work its way under shingles and into seams in the flashing.

Even on steeply sloped roofs, flashing, which covers seams between roofing and chimneys or other protrusions such as skylights or plumbing vent pipes, can be deformed by ice and snow. A piece of metal flashing pulled away from a chimney then acts as a funnel that channels water directly under the roof and into the house.

These connections between different levels and different materi-

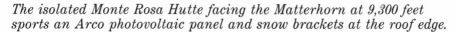

The isolated Monte Rosa Hutte facing the Matterhorn at 9,300 feet sports an Arco photovoltaic panel and snow brackets at the roof edge.

als on the roof are critical. Too often, they are made haphazardly with a piece of aluminum embedded in roofing tar. This is a common weak link on reroofing jobs where a layer of new shingles is laid over a worn layer that already has flashing.

A quick fix can be made by adding roof cement (not roof coating, which is a free-flowing tar) along flashing seams. But this is only a temporary solution. There is only one good way to connect metal flashing to masonry chimneys or to masonry parapet walls surrounding the roof. Approximately ½ inch of mortar between courses (horizontal layers) of brick or block must be chiseled out so that the top edge of the flashing can be folded into the space. After the metal is bent into place, mortar is added to fill the joint and seal the seam from weather.

Another potential bottleneck occurs at the offset fitting between gutters and leaders, an S-shaped piece of pipe that carries water from gutters at roof overhangs back to vertical leaders against the house. Like plumbing traps beneath sinks, these pieces are the first to clog. You can be sure they are clear by flushing the entire downspout system with water while temperatures are above the freezing point or by taking the leader apart to remove accumulated leaves and twigs.

While melting snow must be kept moving into drains, great sheets of ice or clumps of snow that break off from roofs can cause damage and injury. Snow guards, small clips supporting a series of rods like a small fence along the roof edge, can prevent these minor avalanches and permit gradual melting. A less expensive alternative, snow clips (simple wire ties protruding from beneath shingles every few inches) can hold back snow over entryways.

A more elaborate and expensive solution is to install electric resistance-heat wiring in a zigzag pattern along the first few courses of roof shingles. These wires can keep the edge of the roof completely clear and prevent ice dams and damage to gutters and downspouts. But they must be plugged into a waterproof exterior outlet and attached to a thermostat unless you can remember to turn the system on when the snow begins and turn it off later on.

On side walls, where exposure is less of a problem, weak spots above windows and doors can be protected against infiltration by water, ice, and snow with caulking. Flexible silicone caulk works best in these locations, bridging gaps between siding and window or door trim, which swell and shrink at different rates. The silicone has just enough elasticity to accommodate these changes without breaking the weather-tight seam.

Where ice and snow may accumulate at grade level, against masonry foundations, wood siding, or wooden door sills, several precautionary steps can prevent deterioration. First, apply caulk beneath sills and under the lowest course of siding. These joints, out of view and often overlooked during construction, must be closed to keep cold air as well as water out of the house. Also, apply one or more coats of clear wood preservative to wooden sills and to the bottom edges of doors. This is another case of out of sight, out of mind; the end grain, which is most likely to absorb water and lead to swelling and sticking doors, is also the most unprotected edge.

Finally, check downspout outlets, adding short pipe extensions to carry water well away from the foundation. If summer and fall rains have left channels in the ground next to the house, add just enough fill to create a gentle slope away from the foundation to help keep cellars and crawl spaces dry.

JUST ASK

Q The roofer replacing our wood shakes interlaced a roll of asphalt paper with every row. Should this be done to help keep out cold winter wind over our old siding, too?

A According to the Red Cedar Shingle & Handsplit Shake Bureau (Suite 275, 515-116th Ave. NE, Bellevue, WA 98004) asphalt paper is not necessary, although in an old house with a lot of drafts a layer of air-infiltration barrier such as Tyvek house wrap is a sensible extra step. It will not trap moisture in the walls but will stop cold air from leaking through.

Before starting the shingling job, stack up a series of shakes, lapped to the recommended amount of exposure to the weather, and see how the thickest section will fit around existing window and door trim. It may be necessary to add molding to window and door casings and at the building corners to cover the edges of the shakes.

2

COPING WITH WINTER EMERGENCIES

Specialized Gadgets to Help Prevent or Minimize Household Disasters

It's hard to appreciate how much you depend on electricity in a house or apartment until there's a power failure. In some homes a blackout can cut off water, light, heat, and refrigeration, bringing even the most commonplace activities to a halt. But what might turn into a romantic adventure with candles, cold cuts, and tepid beer in the summer can be destructive, costly, and scary in the winter.

The risk of a power failure, fire, or flood increases in winter when ice storms can bring down electrical lines, when wood and coal stoves can spit embers onto a rug, and when low temperatures can rupture plumbing pipes. Winter weather increases not only the risks but also the difficulty of coping with these emergencies. It's hard enough to fix a leaking pipe on a sunny day. It can be nearly impossible at 2:00 A.M. in the cold and dark.

There are many special products available that can prevent or minimize some of the worst problems or at least provide an early warning so you have a chance to limit the damage. Some are so nifty that you must beware of falling prey to the gadget bug. Not that the products are gimmicky in a negative way. But it's easy to get hooked on the inventive mechanical problem solver and to be lulled into a false sense of security by their warning beeps and battery backups.

The most rational way to decide what to buy and how much to spend is to compare the cost of emergency equipment to the cost of repairing or replacing whatever it protects. For example, a $20 smoke alarm that can save lives and a $100,000 house is a bargain, while a $500 emergency generator backing up the power supply to a small refrigerator holding $20 worth of food is overkill.

Instead of the standard list of extra fuses, plenty of candles, and such, here are some of the most unique emergency products and, in their absence, a few suggestions about improvising solutions to house emergencies with the most common tools and materials.

- Emergency Light. No matter what the emergency, you will be able to deal with it faster, more safely, and more efficiently if you can see the problem. Too often the first reaction to an emergency is a maddening search for the one flashlight with good batteries. Tripping over chairs and walking into walls only adds frustration to anxiety, placing you at the mercy of events instead of in control of them.

  The solution is to plug a recharging flashlight into crucially

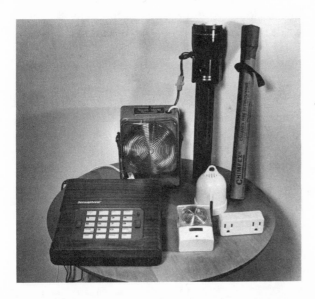

Winter emergency devices include an auto-dialer-monitor, temperature-sensitive lamp, power failure flashlights, and chimney extinguisher.

located electrical outlets (particularly near stairs). When the power goes off, the lights turn on automatically. You can see where you're going and remove the unit from its outlet to use as a portable flashlight. Sanyo's Power Failure Light is about 3½ by 2½ inches and contains a rechargeable nickel cadmium battery that powers the lamp for fifty minutes. (The light retails for approximately $16.)

The Brookstone Thermo Cube controls lights or other appliances by measuring inside air temperature. The device plugs into a grounded outlet, providing thermostatically activated outlets for two appliances (e.g., an auxiliary heater, lamp, electric heat tape to prevent pipe freeze-ups.) Three models, all rated for 1,800 watts, activate the outlets at either 0° F., 20° F., or 35° F. (It retails for approximately $10.)

Working on the same principle, the Eveready Freeze-Up Signal Light is mounted in a window. When its thermostat (on a 20-foot wire) detects a temperature below 45° F., a bright, flashing red light warns a neighbor that the heat is off in your home. The 5-by-5½-inch plastic case needs four D batteries. (It retails for approximately $30.)

Undoubtedly the ultimate flashlight (a $130 rechargeable system with its own ten-page owner's manual), the Mag Instrument commercial-quality model comes with a recharging unit, battery pack, and gripping mount suitable even for cars and boats. The 12¾-inch-long barrel is made of hard, aircraft-type anodized aluminum with a finely knurled surface. A specially coated reflector, lens, and halogen bulb provide over 30,000 candlepower, while a rotating head can adjust the white light to a spot or flood. The intense beam can clearly illuminate a six-foot patch of woods 100 yards away. It's exceptional, and should be for the price.

A portable generator provides the most comprehensive backup for power failures that kill the lights and everything else. Sears offers a variety of generators, from a 750-watt unit ($440) to a 7,500-watt unit ($2,500).

Their 2,100-watt, 5 horsepower, pull-start model with 3-quart fuel tank will run under full load for one and one-half hours, and almost three hours under quarter capacity. The 2,100-watt rating would be enough to keep a small heater, refrigerator, lights, and a few small appliances operational, depending on their specific wattage ratings. (It retails for approximately $650.)

- Water Emergencies. Pipes seem to freeze in cold, dark nooks and crannies, places that are best protected with thermostatically controlled heat tapes. They look like thin extension cords that are spiral wrapped around the pipe. As the temperature falls, a sensor draws current into the wires, which generate enough heat to prevent freezing. Depending on length, heat tapes (or heat cables) may cost $10–$20.

  Prevention is important because emergency pipe repairs often have to wait until the pipe can be thawed and drained. You can't solder a copper pipe filled with water. The pipe won't get hot enough, even though the water boils inside. Pinholes may be plugged with a lead pencil point. Leaks through split pipes can be reduced, if not stopped, by wrapping a piece of rubber or almost any firm but pliable and watertight material over the leak and clamping the patch in place. Adjustable band clamps (the type used on car engine hoses) work well.

  One problem with a pipe leak or broken sump pump is that you may not discover the leak until the furniture starts to float. The Brookstone Sensitive Water Alarm (battery powered and left standing on the floor) sounds an alarm after detecting only .01 inch of water. (It retails for approximately $17.)

- Fire Emergencies. Basic equipment for every home is an ABC-rated fire extinguisher and more smoke alarms for early warning. Any home with a fireplace or wood stove can also benefit from an extinguisher made to fight flue fires, called Chimfex. It's about the size of a large road flare and is struck into ignition on its own cap just as flares are lit. But Chimfex releases a massive volume of gas into the flue (you just toss it into the fire and leave) that will not support combustion. The advantage of Chimfex over liquid extinguishers is that its gases can follow the fire into the flue to reach less accessible hot spots. (It retails for approximately $11.)

One of the most versatile emergency devices is called Sensaphone. It connects to the house wiring and phone line and monitors temperature, noise level, and power-supply status. Accessories can tie in burglar alarms, remote fire detectors, and other devices. The system can be programmed to dial four telephone numbers, automatically and in sequence, until a connection is made. Then a computer-synthesized voice delivers a status report. (For a sample call-in report, dial 800-228-8466.) You can call in for reports, or if one of the parameters you program is exceeded, the system will call you. (Suggested Gulf & Western list price is $249.95, but you can buy Sensaphone for $200 at many outlets.)

For details on the power-failure light, thermocube outlet, freeze-up signal light, Mag recharging flashlight, water-level alarm, and Chimfex extinguisher, write Brookstone Co., 712 Vose Farm Rd., Peterborough, NH 03458. Their catalogs are mailed free on request. For the Sears generator, write Sears Roebuck & Co., Dept. 703, 40–15 Sears Tower, Chicago, IL 60684. For Sensaphone, write Gulf & Western Consumer Electronics, Concord & Tyrens Rds., Aston, PA 19014. The 800-228–8466 sample call-in report clearly demonstrates the machine's features.

JUST ASK

Q A serviceman has suggested a new flame-retention head to improve efficiency (now about 70 percent) of my eighteen-year-old oil furnace. How does the system work, and is it worth the money?

A Flame-retention replacement heads work almost the same way as conventional burners, in which a nozzle sprays an aerated oil mist into the combustion chamber after ignition by a pair of electrodes.

With the add-on retention head, the flame moves down a blast tube toward the combustion chamber but is held in the tube by a concave, finned plate covering most of the outlet. Increased efficiency occurs because oil and air mix evenly, eliminating very rich or very lean concentrations, and because the retained flame promotes afterburning.

Several firms make retention heads that should boost efficiency to 80 or 85 percent. So if the oil bill is $1,000 a year and efficiency increases from 70 to 85 percent (15 percent, or $150 on the bill), the investment should pay for itself in three or four years, depending on labor costs for your particular situation. Up to a seven-year payback is generally considered a worthwhile energy-saving investment.

Check with two or three contractors for estimates and ask your utility company if furnace efficiency is covered by their energy-audit program. Also, you might want to write the Department of Energy, Office of Public Affairs, Washington, DC 20585 for a useful pamphlet, "How to Improve the Efficiency of Your Oil-Fired Furnace."

3

FIGHTING OFF THE ELEMENTS
Working Outside to Protect the Inside

Inside the house, cooking, washing, and the other operations of day-to-day living cause gradual deterioration. Outside, the elements cause decay, particularly water. It seems to find the smallest opening between roof shingles and flashing and soaks into unprotected wood, causing swelling, warping, and rot. Protecting the house against water damage on the outside goes a long way toward minimizing maintenance and repair work on the inside.

• Worn Shingles. Waiting to replace asphalt shingles that show signs of wear is a gamble. Since it is impossible to know exactly when a roof will begin to spring leaks, the best policy is to look for the symptoms of deterioration before the floodgates open. Look for accumulations of shingle stone (the small colored granules embedded in the asphalt surface) at downspout outlets. As more granules are lost, you will notice bare spots of black asphalt. This symptom is hard to miss on shingles with white surface granules.

In the next stage of deterioration, the shingles may cup and

This saltbox makes a traditional and efficient presentation to the weather: three inches of clapboard exposure, small windows, and steep roof.

start to curl away from the roof. This symptom is usually followed by shingle tabs (the exposed section of the shingle) cracking, then breaking altogether. When that happens, nail heads are exposed. If the roof hasn't leaked yet, it will soon.

When only one or two spots on the roof need to be repaired, it may not be necessary to reroof. Of course, working on a roof can be dangerous. The steeper the slope, the greater the risk. So if you have doubts about your equipment or your abilities or you just don't feel right about working up there, don't do it.

To replace a damaged or deteriorated shingle (or group of them), peel away the bad section with a flat-ended pry bar. When you reach the area of good shingles, carefully try to pry up the nails closest to the damaged area. (You'll see that shingles are staggered, so on some courses you will have to reach underneath one shingle to pry up the nail on another.)

With the shingles removed, cut away or lift the tar paper underneath to check for damage on the roof deck. Better to discover any problems now while the roof is exposed and take the extra time to replace rotted boards if necessary. As new shingles are woven back into the staggered pattern, you may not be able to nail the edges where they are covered by existing shingles. In this case, pry the existing shingle up just enough to spread a coat of roof cement (a thick tar) underneath, then press the replacement shingle in place on top of the cement.

• Clogged Gutters and Downspouts. There are two weak links in most gutter and downspout systems. One is a true bottleneck called the elbow or offset fitting—the short, S-shaped section that carries water from the gutter at the roof overhang back against the house, where it connects to a vertical downspout.

Working like a plumbing trap under a kitchen sink, the offset fitting traps leaves, twigs, and other debris washed off the roof and into the gutter. When the gutter appears to be clear and the outlet hole to the downspout is not clogged but water does not drain freely, the downspout should be disassembled and examined. Loosen one side of any straps securing the pipe to the wall and slide the downspout away from the elbow section. Working carefully from the roof, you may be able to clear a blockage with a plumber's snake.

Sometimes debris is packed so tightly that the fitting must be taken apart so you can reach and remove the material. Aside from creating free-flowing drains, it is important to remove compacted leaves trapped at the fitting. They leach tannic acid, which may eventually eat away the metal and cause leaks.

If water is seeping through a loose seam between gutter fittings, apply a thick coat of silicone or butyl caulk to both pieces of metal, press them together so that caulk oozes out of the seam, then secure the joint with pop rivets. Excess silicone can be peeled away after a few hours.

The second weak link in roof drains is the gutter itself. Great pains are taken during construction to keep the rafters in the same plane and to make the overhang form a straight and level line across the side of the house. It looks great. But a flat gutter discourages drainage. And as the building settles, the gutter may actually begin to slope away from the downspout.

It may offend your sense of symmetry, but when drainage is sluggish and the gutter is continually choked with debris, you may have to reinstall the gutter out of level. This is one of the few do-it-yourself jobs that's done right when it looks wrong. Figure about ⅛ inch of slope per running foot, or about 1 inch every 8 feet. On longer lengths, you should be able to get away with a little less slope. On very long runs, say 40 feet or more, slope the gutter away from the center (the highest point) toward a downspout at each end of the house.

• Sticking Windows and Doors. Wood reacts to its environment. In the summer, a wood door will absorb moisture. It may happen gradually as the temperature warms and the humidity increases. A door or window that opens and closes freely may start to scrape or bind on its hinges. To protect against such problems, exterior wood on windows and doors must be protected with paint or some other surface sealer.

But because windows and doors must fit snugly to be energy efficient, there is at least some friction as they operate. That friction scrapes away the protective coating, which leads to more swelling, more friction, and so on, in an increasingly damaging cycle of deterioration. And endless coats of paint applied to protect the wood can eventually build up to such a thickness that a double-hung window, for example, simply can't be budged.

To solve this problem, sand the areas on the edges of the operating parts, the bottom of the door, for example, that have been roughened by friction. (If sanding the rough spots and tightening hinges does not allow free operation, it may be necessary to plane or heavily sand the few remaining high spots.) Apply at least one coat of penetrating sealer to protect the wood fibers, then a coat of paint of other surface sealer. Don't forget the bottom edge of the door—it's the most difficult to get at but also the most susceptible to swelling. It may be necessary to take the door off its hinges to work on the bottom edge.

Sand down and seal the bottom edge, then mount a piece of precut U-shaped flashing around it. This prevents the edge in closest contact with the ground from soaking up water like a sponge. Several types of flashing can be used, including a rigid, U-shaped section on the door that fits against a matching piece fitted to or replacing a conventional sill.

JUST ASK

Q I recently found a long crack in the stuccoed foundation running from the bottom of the siding to the ground. Since the surface stucco is holding, how can I tell if there is structural or only cosmetic damage?

A You're right to make this distinction. All buildings settle a bit, often enough to crack plaster or stucco but not the concrete or block underneath. Even old buildings may begin to shift if, for example, foundation drains become clogged so that groundwater erodes soil around foundation footings.

First, check inside the cellar or crawl space to see if the crack runs through the wall. If it doesn't show inside, chances are the crack is only cosmetic. Next, determine if the crack is old or new. Old cracks have edges rounded by the weather, hold dust, dirt, and debris from insects, and show traces of any recent painting. New cracks have sharp edges and a color different from surrounding painted surfaces; they may still be growing and need to be monitored.

To do this, draw two parallel lines, one on each side of the crack. Measure the distance between the marks precisely. If the crack has shifted ⅛ inch or more when you recheck the marks in about 6 months, settling is under way. In most cases 1–1½ inches total settlement can be tolerated safely. But if movement continues after obvious drainage problems are corrected, it may be necessary to reexcavate and shore up the foundation—a costly and time-consuming job.

4

IMPROVING THE EFFICIENCY OF WOOD-BURNING STOVES

Catalytic Combustors Increase Heat Output, Reduce Pollutants

One small piece of equipment has revolutionized wood heating. Overlooked by many wood-stove manufacturers until this season, it improves heat output while reducing exhaust pollutants and creosote buildup.

Corning's catalytic combustor is a thick, honeycomb-shaped wafer through which smoke passes on its way to the chimney. Special coatings on the wafer spark a complex series of chemical changes in the smoke, "cracking it," as the Corning engineers explain the process, into particles that can be reburned. The secondary combustion takes place inside the stove, producing heat where it's needed and using up ingredients in the smoke that otherwise would contribute to air pollution and the possibility of a chimney fire.

The name catalytic combustor may bring to mind a related product, the catalytic converter used on the exhaust systems of automobiles to clean up emissions. As car enthusiasts know, exhaust is cleaned at the expense of acceleration and power. But there seem to be no negative trade-offs with the catalytic combustor.

Early tests conducted by Corning and independent labs showed that the use of a combustor led to a 20 percent increase in heat output, a 75 percent reduction in exhaust pollutants, and a 95 percent (Corning claims only 90 percent) burn of creosote-producing gases. Corning has confirmed even better results from tests on the latest generation of airtight wood stoves that are specifically designed around the combustor. While the 90 percent figure for creosote reduction still holds, there is a 90 percent reduction in exhaust pollutants and up to a 50 percent increase in heat output. If you burned four cords of wood last year, you could install an airtight, combustor-equipped stove this year that would deliver the same heat from less than three cords.

With such impressive numbers it is difficult to understand why so many manufacturers waited several years before including the combustor in one or more standard stove models. Maybe they had

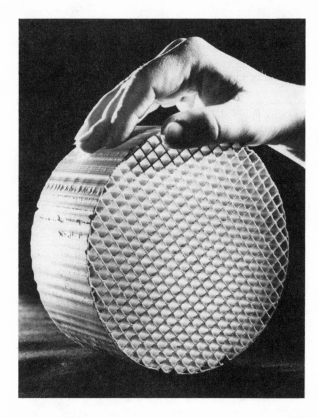

Corning's catalytic combustor increases heating efficiency while reducing creosote buildup and air pollution by reburning exhaust gases.

the same reaction as many consumers—that it seemed to good to be true. More serious concerns centered upon the combustor's durability and a basic safety question: What happens if the honeycomb becomes clogged?

Corning's tests on actual wood-stove installations now predict an operational life of about twelve thousand hours. In upper New York State, where a stove might burn day and night, every day, over a four-month heating season, the combustor would last roughly four years. In Virginia, where more moderate temperatures might dictate that a stove run twenty-four hours a day, twenty days a month, over a three-month heating season, the combustor would last roughly eight years.

Clogging is another matter. The catalytic honeycomb passages are rather small, so that ash or a piece of paper used to start the fire could reduce the flow of smoke, even block it completely. To operate efficiently and safely, combustors should be located close to the wood fire and used only in conjunction with a safety bypass and other design features. Add-on combustors for existing wood stoves cannot meet this test. Some fit into the stove flue pipe, others into a specially made boxlike section of flue pipe that contains a bypass and is designed to disperse the additional heat produced at the combustor. Combustor temperatures may well reach over 1,000° F. No flue pipe is made to withstand that kind of heat or to exchange anywhere near the full potential for usable BTUs sealed in the exhaust system. I asked Corning for referrals to add-on combustor manufacturers. They declined.

However, they will refer consumer inquiries to stove manufacturers who have successfully incorporated the combustor into an airtight design. Adding a combustor is not like fiddling with a fender design to create a new-model car. It's like building a completely different kind of car. Airtight combustor stoves offer an excellent alternative to typical wood-burning fireplaces. While old, reasonably efficient Colonial fireplaces were shallow, with tall openings and a back wall slanted toward the room to reflect heat, most modern fireplaces are deep, with smaller openings. The modern design prevents smoke from escaping into the room but loses 50 to 60 percent of the heat up the chimney. Owners of standard (nonairtight) wood stoves might also consider upgrading to a combustor-equipped model; the investment would be well worth the money.

New technology may have revolutionized wood-stove efficiency, but the other half of the combustion equation, the fuel, is unchanged. A log is still a log. Combustor reburning can squeeze most of the potential heat from wood, and airtights can prolong the combustion to minimize tending and refueling. But wood has a limited amount of heat to give up. To maximize heat production, avoid wet wood and carefully select the type of wood you burn.

Wet does not mean left out in the rain, although that doesn't help. Wet means green, recently cut wood with roughly an 80 percent moisture content. Department of Energy tests show that 15 percent of the potential heat in green wood is lost in evaporation. (Energy once used to convert the moisture cannot be recaptured.)

After it's cut, wood dries out and seasons as it ages, opening telltale cracks, called checking, at the ends of the logs. On average, after only three months of air drying, the moisture content is down to 35 or 40 percent. After six months, it's reduced to 30 percent, then to 25 percent after one year. At this low level, only 4 percent of the heat is used to evaporate moisture. Seasoning can't add BTUs to the logs, but it does mean more of the BTUs will be converted to usable heat.

Some woods offer more heat than others simply by packing more wood into the log. Soft woods such as pine and spruce have more space between the wood fibers and are lighter than hardwoods such as oak and maple. While the BTUs per pound of wood do not vary much from softwoods (spruce has about 8,750 BTUs per pound) to hardwoods (red oak has about 8,700), the BTU rating per cord (a 4-by-4-by-8-foot stack measured by volume, not weight) does.

It may help to think of softwood as a neatly packed suitcase in which the contents have plenty of room and hardwood as a duffel bag of the same size crammed with two suitcases' worth of clothes. One cord of white pine produces about 14 million BTUs; hemlock and spruce about 15 million. But a cord of maple produces about 21 million BTUs; white oak, 23 million; and hickory, 25 million.

Wood species and seasoning time determine the true amount of potential heat supplied to a stove. Improved wood-stove technology can now use that fuel very efficiently, reinforcing wood as a legitimate heating alternative to oil, gas, and electricity. In addition to a referral list of combustor-equipped stove manufacturers, Corning has produced a well-illustrated booklet on the catalytic combustor. Write Corning Catalytic Combustor, MP-21-1, Corning Glass Works, Corning, NY 14831.

JUST ASK

Q How can I prevent the heavy buildup of snow and icicles from damaging the roof and gutter system?

A Once snow and ice are on the roof, it is difficult to take preventive measures. First, working safely from a ladder (and this requires special caution during bad weather), break off the icicles before they weigh down the gutter and literally rip it off the roof. If you can get at the roof edge from a dormer window, for example, consider pouring hot water on the roof to melt ice accumulated in gutters and downspouts.

Freeze/thaw cycles that occur when the sun begins to melt snow accumulations (which then turn to slush and freeze at night) can destroy the edge of a roof. Clear off as much snow and ice as you can without hacking at the roof or poking holes in the shingles. Let the sun take care of the rest.

Looking ahead to next winter, think about installing heat tapes in a zigzag pattern along the last few courses of shingles. These devices, which look like extension cords, draw just enough current to produce heat. That is often enough to prevent ice dams, snow buildup, and many problems associated with a stopped-up gutter and downspout system.

INDEX